D0476936

A
Pocket Guide
to
Musicals

Library Learning Information

To renew this item call:

020 7364 4332
or visit
www.ideastore.co.uk

TOWER HAMLETS

Created and managed by Tower Hamlets Council

WITHDRAWN

A Pocket Guide to Musicals

Maureen Hughes

REMEMBER WHEN

First published in Great Britain in 2008 by
REMEMBER WHEN
An imprint of
Pen & Sword Books Ltd
47 Church Street
Barnsley
South Yorkshire
S70 2AS

Copyright © Maureen Hughes, 2008

ISBN 978 1 84468 039 9

The right of Maureen Hughes to be identified as Author of this work
has been asserted by her in accordance with the Copyright, Designs
and Patents Act 1988.

A CIP catalogue record for this book is available from the British
Library

All rights reserved. No part of this book may be reproduced or trans-
mitted in any form or by any means, electronic or mechanical including
photocopying, recording or by any information storage and retrieval
system, without permission from the Publisher in writing.

Typeset by Phoenix Typesetting, Auldgirth, Dumfriesshire
Printed and bound by CPI UK

Pen & Sword Books Ltd incorporates the Imprints of Pen & Sword
Aviation, Pen & Sword Maritime, Pen & Sword Military, Wharncliffe
Local History, Pen & Sword Select, Pen & Sword Military Classics, Leo
Cooper, Remember When, Seaforth Publishing and Frontline Publishing

For a complete list of Pen & Sword titles please contact
PEN & SWORD BOOKS LIMITED
47 Church Street, Barnsley, South Yorkshire, S70 2AS, England
E-mail: enquiries@pen-and-sword.co.uk
Website: www.pen-and-sword.co.uk

For My Children
Kieran & Vicky

LONDON BOROUGH TOWER HAMLETS	
C001591250	
HJ	13/08/2008
792.6	£9.99
WHID	

Contents

Foreword

*Think of musical comedy; the
most glorious words
in the English language*

Richard Jordan, producer

THESE are the words that Julian Marsh spits out with such passion in the musical *42nd Street* that it makes your heart tingle with excitement – well, mine anyway – and, as a result, Peggy Sawyer does not turn her back on Broadway and boards the train back to Allen Town.

Although *42nd Street* is a work of fiction, it is the sentiment so clearly reflected by Marsh's comment which perhaps best illustrates the drive that powers an industry, and its remarkable individuals, who in their attempts – often against considerable odds – devote months, years, even lives to try and make their idea and dream for a musical come to life.

The creator of a musical is just as determined as any inventor, because that is essentially what they are, only their invention is a four-dimensional living and breathing thing, fuelled on belief, risk and energy – with ultimately the audience powering the engine.

But, like any invention, the odds are enormous and, while the rewards can be huge, the failings are extreme and public. Perhaps a life in the theatre would be easier if you could do it without having a heart, because it gets broken many times. However, that would not make the extraordinarily creative individuals you meet throughout your career – and throughout this book – survive. What a career in theatre has taught me, and what this book reflects, is that by watching, listening and learning from so many great theatre makers, to succeed in theatre you need a lot of courage, talent, self-belief, trust, and above all, optimism. Because, for every *Cats*, there's a *Carrie*, for every *Wicked*, there's a *Which Witch*.

In the world of musical theatre, unlike straight drama, its flops are nearly as legendary as its hits. Much of this is down to cost, with *Lord of the Rings* taking musical theatre budgets to the highest in musical theatre history. That means that, more than ever before, the stakes are dangerously high for any commercial musical. That can make it a great height from which to fall but, equally, if you get the formula right, then the lifespan of a musical is multi-global, and with enormous returns. But, from my own producing experience, for those at the grass roots of today's musical theatre – the writers – it is not the pay cheque that is their primary driving force, but the hunger of an idea, which consumes them night and day in a way that their life depends on it, with the overwhelming need to present that on a stage somewhere. I often think that, for a composer and lyricist writing a musical, it must be a lot like being a mole – you tunnel in the dark for a long time and, every so often, come up for a bit of light, before going back under, into the dark again to tunnel a bit further – certainly producing can also be like that!

Within the pages of this book, you will meet some of the people who create the music and the words, and others who bring them to life. Good theatre is about collaboration and, whilst each person's experience and journey to making a musical is unique and intensely personal to them, they all share certain common characteristics in their individual quests.

Alongside a great score and production values, much of the success of a musical can simply be down to the luck of the right timing. Who knows if *Cats* would work if it opened today, but its arrival in 1981 came at the point when there was nothing else like it around and it made people sit up and pay attention. Those working in musical theatre are certainly pioneers. Go back to the *Student Prince* via, for example, *Miss Saigon*, *Les Misérables*, *Company*, *Sweeney Todd*, *Tommy*, *Little Shop of Horrors*, *Evita*, *Jesus Christ Superstar*, *Cabaret*, *Hair*, *Guys and Dolls*, *Carousel*, *Of Thee I Sing*, *The Boyfriend*, *Show Boat* and watch out for the pointers that have influenced a profession and continue to do so today – Jonathan Larson's influences for *Rent* are just as rooted in Verdi and Hammerstein as they are in modern America. It's the skill of these individuals in having a good idea, and then the ability and belief to be able to weave that into something that is coherent and relevant to today's musical theatre industry and audiences, which makes these people the extraordinary pioneers of today's musical theatre. Just like their own mentors, they are influencing tomorrow's musical theatre because, somewhere, there is a young man or woman listening on their iPod to *Rent*, *Spring Awakening*, *Wicked* or *South Pacific* and thinking that they too have a good idea which empowers and consumes them with an overwhelming need to launch it on an unsuspecting world.

For those of us working in today's theatre industry, we are lucky to be in a business where you never stop learning; the only way you get to keep knowledge is to share it – the pages of this book help to do exactly that.

Every time I watch or listen to a musical I have the chance to step into a world within a world with its own reality. A world in which, with its great musical theatres, theatre can reach out and touch hands with you like no other art form.

Richard Jordan,
Producer

Chapter One

Welcome to the World of Musical Theatre

THE CREATIVE TREE

Composer & Lyricist & Librettist
The writers must find a Producer willing to 'option' their work

Producer
The Producer must raise the money, generally from his angels; he must then select his Director

Director
Together with the Producer, the Director will select the creative team who will make the above creatives' vision come to life on the stage

Sound Designer — **Lighting Designer** — **Casting Director** — **Choreographer** — **Costume Designer** — **Set Designer**

A team of light techs & operators

Assistants

Carpenters & labourers

Dancers

A team of sound techs & operators

Assistants & pianist

Wardrobe Master/Mistress

Performers

Seamstresses & Assistants

Musical Director

Musicians

Introduction

FOR THOSE who truly love the stage and all that goes with it, musicals are quite simply an important and invaluable member of the thespian family. Sadly, however, there are those who succumb to a form of aesthetic snobbery and believe that musicals are at best trite or, at worst, a cultural desert where the only oasis in sight is the end of the show; for them, the musical is the black sheep of the thespian family, the wayward aunt, the out-spoken cousin, the rebellious brother, the one who should never be let into the inner sanctum of this family fold.

Whatever your personal view, interest in musical theatre has never been greater both on this side of the pond and the other. The West End is alive with the 'sound of music' and TV constantly entertains us with reality shows as they search for the next performer with the *X Factor*, the next leading lady in a musical, the next winner of a dance fevered programme; on and on it goes.

My own love affair with the musical began many years ago. In fact, with hindsight and the wisdom of age, I can actually pinpoint that my pull into the theatre began long before I was even five years old.

My parents were house hunting and I can vividly remember trying to persuade them to buy various houses simply because they had a bay window. You see, I thought that a bay window with curtains straight across instead of around the bay would make a wonderful stage. I'm not sure where I thought my obviously 'very tiny' actors and actresses were going to make their entrances and exits, but I didn't care, all I saw was a stage. Eventually, and to my great disappointment, my parents settled on a house without my inbuilt stage, but I adapted and created an outdoor theatre on a square piece of concrete in front of a garden shed. Even better, because now I not only had a stage but a backstage area too – in the form of the shed which also served as a dressing room and which came with a ready supply of first night flowers, usually in plant pots, but I didn't care!

I created so many productions on that piece of concrete that I think my parents often regretted not buying a house with a bay window, because not even the weather was allowed to stop my next blockbuster. So that was my starting point, although I obviously didn't know this at the time because, whenever anyone asked me what I wanted to be when I grew up, I would always tell them that I wanted to be a fashion designer! It remains a great mystery to me why I would say such a thing as my drawing skills were and are very limited and my fashion sense is non-existent, and remains so today, as my friends will vouch! However, my parents said nothing; they neither pushed nor encouraged me in either direction, but just let me get on with creating theatre for them, an assortment of dolls and a few of my reluctant friends who, incidentally, thought my obsession with shows to be decidedly odd.

Time marched on and my passion for the theatre – and, in particular, musical theatre – never abated, but instead became my life and my career as I have written eight musicals and teach musical theatre in a vocational school; a career which has now spanned almost 40 years (and yes I was teaching this 'subject' long before it became fashionable!).

During this time I have read innumerable books on teaching and even more on musicals, and what has always struck me is that so many of them, I am sad to say, have little about what the reader actually wants to know, so much so that I didn't even finish many of them! In a rather convoluted way, they seemed to take so long to get to the point that by the time they actually did, I had lost interest. I want this book to be different; I want it to be accessible and an easy read for everyone who enjoys watching a musical. If you want to know from which musical a song originated, then it is simple to look up, as is the decade in which a musical made its first appearance; you might want to know whether a particular musical was a film or a stage musical first – another easy search. There is also a straight-forward timeline for some of the more well-known creators of musicals and some interesting, little known facts about various aspects of this wonderful art form. It's all here and it's all easy to find and easy to read. In fact, I want the reader to feel that they know me as someone they feel they can actually hear. I am told by my family that they know when I am enjoying a book because I start talking to the page and arguing with the words – so I'll be listening out for you!

When the reader closes my book after the final page I want them to think, 'Wow! I never realised that', then go out, buy a ticket for a musical and watch it through different eyes; through more knowledgeable eyes.

Maureen Hughes

So let the show begin

A Recipe for Success

There is a plan, a strategy – a recipe – behind every success story and contrary to that time old saying, success does not come to he who *waits*; it comes to he who *works*. But as with all good recipes there must be some basic ingredients.

Take a Large Helping of Music

The style can vary; it can be rock, pop, opera, folk, jazz, contemporary – any style at all; it can be original, it can be 'borrowed', as it was in the Eighteenth Century. There are no rules; you just need music.

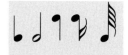

Add Some Colourful Words

You have the melody, so now add some words; words to tell a story, to portray an emotion; to tell everyone what has just happened, or is going to happen; powerful words to drive the plot forward. You now have a song.

There's no business like show business

Mix in a Dance Routine

Most musicals have dance as a part of their recipe; a dance routine can give us a visual feel for the underlying emotion of the piece.

Stir Vigorously and add to an Outstanding and Gripping Storyline

Take all of the above and mix it into the story, commonly called the plot and generally recognised as the most important ingredient of all. A strong storyline will keep the audience enthralled and receptive to the incomparable art form of:

Musical Theatre

Poor Man's Theatre?

So exactly what is musical theatre? Well, what the theatrical snobs amongst us will try to convince you of is that it is 'not real theatre', that it is, in fact, a 'poor man's theatre', theatre for the intellectually inferior. So what do I think to that? I think there is nothing 'poor' about Lord Andrew Lloyd-Webber, or about Sir Cameron Mackintosh; not in any sense of the word. I think that they are both artistically rich . . . and of course financially not too badly off either! They are both men for whom I have the greatest of respect, and both are Masters in the art of musical theatre.

My advice to you then is that when someone laughs at you for enjoying a musical – and trust me they will – point out that *they* are obviously in the minority, for without the support of the theatre-going majority, neither of these two gentlemen would be so successful, nor would musical theatre be so successful. In fact, theatre itself would be so much the poorer. Tell them to take a look at the West End and Broadway where so often musicals dominate.

Watching a musical is also quite simply a wonderful way to spend an evening, be it as a producer, a performer, a member of the creative team or as a member of the audience. In my view, there is nothing to rival this, one of the greatest and oldest of art forms, which we can trace as far back as the Ancient Greeks.

To create a musical, masters in this specific form of art are required, including composers; lyricists/librettists; producers; choreographers; casting directors; directors; musical directors; musical arrangers; set designers; lighting designers; sound designers; musicians; costume designers. Take a look at the programme from any musical and you will soon see just how extensive the list of the creative team involved can be.

Once we have the experts in place, who are at the very core and form the foundation of musical theatre, then, and only then, can the search begin for the performers who will breathe life into the piece. And finding performers to do this is not an easy task when casting a musical, for generally speaking the search will be on for a 'triple threat artist'. That is, an artist who can sing, dance and act to an incredibly high standard, for the art of musical theatre is the marriage of three disciplines, singing, dancing and acting. Being able to do just one of these is amazing in itself, but to be accomplished in all three is in fact amazing – and essential.

So, is musical theatre really a 'poor man's theatre'? I think not. I think it is quite the opposite; it is an artistically rich member of the theatrical world.

The Trio of Grand Masters

As stated earlier, and for reasons that I have never fully understood, musical theatre is often ridiculed and maligned by those who consider it to be for the less intelligent of theatre goers. To those people, I would like to ask the following questions:

Q. Is it easier to write a theatrical piece which includes music and lyrics in addition to the book?

A. No, of course it isn't!

Q. Is it easier for a producer to 'gather together a several million pound investment from his angels' to mount a musical production than it is to 'gather together a few hundred thousand' to mount a play?

A. No, of course it isn't!

Q. Is it easier for a director to think about incorporating the additional elements of song and dance into his masterpiece, than just the spoken word?

A. No, of course it isn't!

Q. Why then is it considered by the 'superior thespians' a mortal sin to enjoy theatre which they feel is devoid of any emotional depth and which is in no way thought provoking – theatre which they feel cannot improve or change the world? Why do they consider it a mortal sin to go to the theatre to simply enjoy oneself, or even worse, escape from the realities of a difficult world? And why can't theatre goers simply choose what they want to see without being made to feel inferior if they choose to see a musical?

A. Any answers gratefully received!

Musicals are here to stay and the public will go on enjoying them, if not always being educated by them! Take a look at the West End and you will find – with the exception of *The Mousetrap*, of course – that the longest running shows are musicals; these are the shows that the public want to see. And behind many of these shows we will find one of **The Trio of Grand Masters**, Lord Lloyd-Webber, Sir Cameron Mackintosh or Sir Trevor Nunn; if we are lucky maybe all three, such as in the case of *Cats* where Lord Lloyd-Webber wrote the music, Sir Trevor Nunn directed it and Sir Cameron Mackintosh produced it!

All three of these masters have been honoured with titles in recognition of their contribution to theatre – *to musical theatre*. But guess what, they are not unintelligent gentlemen, as many not 'into' musical theatre would have us believe; in fact they are quite the opposite as you will soon discover.

Lord Andrew Lloyd-Webber

MAJOR SHOWS

Joseph and the Amazing Technicolor Dreamcoat (1968) • *Jesus Christ Superstar* (1971) • *Evita* (1978) • *Cats* (1981) • *Song and Dance* (1982) • *Starlight Express* (1984) • *The Phantom of the Opera* (1986) • *Aspects of Love* (1989) • *Sunset Boulevard* (1993) • *Whistle Down the Wind* (1996) • *The Beautiful Game* (2000) • *The Woman in White* (2004)

MAJOR SONGS

Any Dream Will Do (*Joseph and the Amazing Technicolor Dreamcoat*) • I Don't Know How to Love Him (*Jesus Christ Superstar*) • Another Suitcase in Another Hall, Don't Cry for Me Argentina, You Must Love Me (*Evita*) • Memory (*Cats*) • The Music of the Night (*The Phantom of the Opera*) • Love Changes Everything (*Aspects of Love*) • With One Look, As If We Never Said Goodbye (*Sunset Boulevard*) • No Matter What (*Whistle Down the Wind*)

THE MAJOR MILESTONES ON ANDREW LLOYD-WEBBER'S MUSICAL JOURNEY

1948 Andrew is born into a musical family, the first son of William Lloyd Webber, Director of the London College of Music and Jean Johnstone, a piano teacher. At this stage, there is no hyphen in his name.

1951 Julian, Andrew's younger brother is born; he is set to become a celebrated cellist later in life.

1953 At only five years of age, Andrew is already playing the piano; he later goes up to Oxford to read history, which he eventually abandons for a career in music.

1965 Andrew receives a letter from Tim Rice, who is looking to collaborate with a composer, and the renowned partnership is formed.

1968 A 15-minute version of *Joseph and the Amazing Technicolor Dreamcoat* has its first performance at Colet Court School in Hammersmith, London. As a result, a relationship is forged between David Land and the pair of young

Lord Andrew Lloyd-Webber
Born: 22 March 1948

writers, who are then paid £3,000 per year to write a new musical – a fortune in the 1960s. *Jesus Christ Superstar* is the result.

1970 *Jesus Christ Superstar* concept album is released.

1971 *Jesus Christ Superstar* opens on Broadway.

1972 Andrew marries Sarah Jane Hugill, with whom he goes on to have two children.

1972 *Jesus Christ Superstar* opens in the West End.

1973 The film version of *Jesus Christ Superstar* is released.

1975 *Jeeves* opens in the West End – it is not a success which is a rare occurrence for Andrew.

1976 'Don't Cry for Me Argentina', from the yet to be released stage musical *Evita,* is released as a single.

1976 Andrew forms The Really Useful Company.

1978 *Evita* opens in the West End.

1978 Andrew's composition, *Variations,* becomes the theme tune for *The South Bank Show.*

1979 *Evita* opens on Broadway after first playing Los Angeles and San Francisco.

1980 A concert performance of *Tell Me on a Sunday* plays in London.

1981 *Cats,* Andrew's musical in which he sets music to T.S. Eliot's poems from *Old Possum's Book Of Practical Cats*, opens in the West End.

1982 *Song and Dance* opens in the West End.

1982 *Cats* the musical opens on Broadway.

1982 *Joseph and the Amazing Technicolor Dreamcoat* opens on Broadway.

1983 Andrew buys his first theatre, the Palace Theatre, in the West End of London.

1984 Following his divorce from Sarah Jane Hugill in 1983, he marries the soprano Sarah Brightman.

1984 *Starlight Express* opens in the West End.

1985 *Song and Dance* opens on Broadway.

1986 A short musical entitled *Cricket*, which Andrew wrote together with Tim Rice to celebrate the Queen's 60th birthday, is premièred in Windsor.

1986 *The Phantom of the Opera* opens in the West End with Andrew's wife, Sarah Brightman, playing the lead role of Christine.

1987 *Starlight Express* opens on Broadway.

1988 *The Phantom of the Opera* opens on Broadway.

1989 *Aspects of Love* opens in the West End

1990 *Aspects of Love* opens on Broadway.

1991 Now divorced from Sarah Brightman, Andrew marries Madeline Gurdon with whom he goes on to have three children.

1992 Andrew Lloyd Webber receives a knighthood and becomes Sir Andrew Lloyd-Webber.

1993 *Sunset Boulevard* opens in the West End.

1994 *Sunset Boulevard* opens on Broadway after first playing Los Angeles.

1996 The World Première of *By Jeeves* (a reworking of the 1975 show *Jeeves*) opens at the Stephen Joseph Theatre, Scarborough, UK (Alan Ayckbourn, who wrote the book and lyrics for the show, is the Artistic Director of the Stephen Joseph Theatre).

1996 The film version of *Evita* – starring Madonna – is released.

1996 *Whistle Down the Wind* premières in Washington USA.

1997 Andrew Lloyd Webber is invested into the House of Lords as Lord Lloyd-Webber of Sydmonton in the County of Berkshire. (Note the hyphenated surname, unlike his commoner surname).

1998 Lord Andrew Lloyd-Webber's 50th Birthday Celebration Concert is held at the Royal Albert Hall, London.

1998 *Whistle Down the Wind* opens in the West End.

2000 *The Beautiful Game* opens in the West End

9

2001 *By Jeeves* opens in the West End.

2002 *Cats* closes in the West End – 21 years after it first opened.

2004 *The Woman in White* opens in the West End.

2004 The film version of *The Phantom of the Opera* premières in London.

2006 Andrew becomes an unexpected TV star when in a new reality TV show – *How Do You Solve a Problem Like Maria?* – he searches for a female to take the lead role in *The Sound of Music*, a show he is about to produce in the West End. The public take to Andrew in a way no one could have predicted and he is officially declared: 'A thoroughly nice chap'.

2007 He repeats the winning formula of using the reality TV approach to find a star to take the lead in another show, but this time it is in one of his own shows, *Joseph and His Amazing Technicolor Dreamcoat*, and again he becomes a darling of the public.

2007 Andrew is in demand throughout the world to repeat his successful reality TV formula.

2007 *Whistle Down the Wind* begins a US tour.

2008 Andrew searches for a Nancy and Oliver on the reality TV show, *I'd Do Anything* for Sir Cameron Mackintosh's production of *Oliver* in the West End.

2008 Andrew is awarded an outstanding achievement prize at the Classical BRIT awards.

OVERVIEW

In my opinion, Lord Lloyd-Webber is without doubt the greatest contributor to musical theatre of both this and the last century. He is also known as a prolific producer, not only of his own works but of the works of others too, and not only musicals. These include: *Daisy Pulls It Off*, *The Hired Man*, *Lend Me a Tenor*, *Bombay Dreams* and *On Your Toes*; and, he has also produced the film version of his own musical *The Phantom of the Opera* and owns many West End theatres, including the Palace Theatre.

Like his one time collaborator, Tim Rice, his interests are wider and more far reaching than just theatre alone. For example, Andrew has an extensive art collection – as well as an impressive cellar of vintage wine.

He is not only recognised by his own country as a great artistic talent, but was officially recognised by the USA in December 2006 when he received a Kennedy Center Honor, one of the highest awards for achievement in the arts in that country.

Andrew frequently holds the Sydmonton Arts Festival at his Berkshire country home, where a variety of exclusive previews are performed before an invited and exclusive audience from the world of theatre, film and television. The purpose of this festival is to gauge the future commercial viability of new works; in fact, Andrew frequently shows his own new works to this privileged audience. An invitation to this event is a much coveted 'prize' and one to be treasured as much as any award.

Lord Andrew Lloyd-Webber has written no fewer than 15 musicals at the time of going to press and is currently working on his 16th; no book, however, could ever hope to keep up with the genius of this extraordinary man. The list is currently as follows:

ASPECTS OF LOVE, 1989

Collaborator: Don Black and Charles Hart
The song 'Love Changes Everything' was released as a single and proved to be a hit for Michael Ball.
Synopsis: The story of the complications that entangled love affairs can create.

BEAUTIFUL GAME (THE), 2000

Collaborator: Ben Elton
'Let Us Love in Peace' from the musical was the closing song at the service for families of the World Trade Center atrocity in October 2001.
Synopsis: It is a story of ordinary teenagers in love and is based around the 'beautiful game' of football.

BY JEEVES, 1996

Collaborator: Alan Ayckbourn
The precursor to this musical was entitled *Jeeves* and opened at Her Majesty's Theatre in the West End in 1975 – it was not a success.
Synopsis: This is a farcical tale using the basic plot of a play within a play.

CATS, 1981

Collaborator: Based on the poems of T.S. Eliot
To date, over 150 artists have recorded the song 'Memory'.
Synopsis: Set on a rubbish dump where all the cats meet for the Jellicle Ball and during which one will be awarded an extra life.

EVITA, 1978

Collaborator: Tim Rice
'Don't Cry for Me Argentina', was released prior to the show by Julie Covington and sold over 2 million copies.

Synopsis: The story of a poor Argentinian girl's rise from the gutter to be the spiritual leader of her country partly based on the true story of Eva Peron.

JESUS CHRIST SUPERSTAR, 1970
Collaborator: Tim Rice
This musical opened in the USA before it opened in the UK.
Synopsis: The story of the last seven days in the life of Christ as seen through the eyes of Judas.

JOSEPH AND THE AMAZING TECHNICOLOR DREAMCOAT, 1982
Collaborator: Tim Rice
The first performance at Colet Court School in Hammersmith was just a 15-minute long cantata.
Synopsis: The biblical story of Joseph, his technicolour coat and his dreams.

LIKES OF US (THE), 1965
Collaborator: Tim Rice
Although composed in 1965, it was not performed until 2005 when a production was staged at Lloyd Webber's Sydmonton Festival.
Synopsis: A musical telling the true story of Dr Bernardo.

PHANTOM OF THE OPERA (THE), 1986
Collaborator: Charles Hart (additional lyrics by Richard Stilgoe)
Andrew's second wife, Sarah Brightman, played the lead part of Christine in the original West End production.
Synopsis: A young singer is having lessons from a mysterious singing teacher – the Phantom – who is insanely possessive.

SONG AND DANCE, 1985
Collaborator: Don Black
Variations – a piece in this show – was composed by Andrew for his younger cellist brother Julian, and is a set of variations on the famous *A Minor Caprice No. 24* by Paganini.
Synopsis: The first half of the show is dance and the second half is song, hence the title: *Song and Dance*.

STARLIGHT EXPRESS, 1987
Collaborator: Richard Stilgoe and Don Black

There is a special skate school where new cast members train to roller skate.
Synopsis: The story of steam versus electric is played out on roller skates.

SUNSET BOULEVARD, 1993
Collaborator: Don Black and Christopher Hampton
A musical which is based on an old black and white film of the same name.
Synopsis: A faded star is trying to make a comeback 'aided' by a self-obsessed struggling writer.

TELL ME ON A SUNDAY, 1980
Collaborator: Don Black
Originally half of the show *Song and Dance* before being developed into a show in its own right.
Synopsis: The story of a young English Girl in New York as she searches for love.

WHISTLE DOWN THE WIND, 1996
Collaborator: John Steinman
On the West End opening night, Lottie Mayor was in fact 24 years old when she played the part of the young 15-year-old, Swallow. The original novel was written by Mary Hayley Bell, wife of Sir John Mills and Hayley Mills, their daughter, starred in the original film.
Synopsis: A 15-year-old girl believes that Jesus Christ is hiding in a barn and she vows to protect him.

WOMAN IN WHITE (THE), 2004
Collaborator: David Zippel
The original novel was written by Wilkie Collins, who was a close friend of Charles Dickens.
Synopsis: A Victorian thriller of love, betrayal and greed with the pivotal character being the mysterious 'Woman in White', adding another essential ingredient – mystery.

Sir Cameron Mackintosh

1946 Born in Enfield, London, the son of a Scottish father and a Maltese mother, Cameron is educated at Prior Park College, Bath.

1954 At just eight years of age, Cameron is taken to see the musical *Salad Days* and his ambition, desire and need to produce is born, later prompting him to drop out of the Central School of Speech and

Drama and take a more practical approach to realising his dream. He starts his professional life as a stage-hand at Drury Lane.

1966 He is appointed Assistant Stage Manager on the National tour of *Oliver!*

1973 Cameron produces his first original musical, *The Card,* written by husband and wife team Tony Hatch and Jackie Trent.

1976 He produces the international hit, *Side by Side by Sondheim.*

1980 He collaborates with Tom Lehrer on a revue of his songs called *Tomfoolery.*

Sir Cameron Mackintosh
Born: 17 October 1946

1980 Andrew Lloyd Webber suggests that the pair work together, and so a partnership that will be repeated over the years, and is set to shape the future of musical theatre, is formed.

1981 Cameron produces Andrew Lloyd Webber's new, and at that time both ground-breaking and controversial, musical *Cats*; he is now well and truly, on his way to becoming the highly respected producer we know today.

1985 As co-producer with the Royal Shakespeare Company (RSC), Cameron produces the musical *Les Misérables*, which first opens at the Barbican in London before transferring to the Palace Theatre in the West End.

1986 Cameron joins Andrew Lloyd Webber again, this time to produce *The Phantom of the Opera*, which opens in the West End.

1987 Cameron's production of Stephen Sondheim and James Goldman's *Follies* opens in the West End.

1989 His production, *Miss Saigon* opens in Drury Lane. This is the second show he has produced for the French writing team Claude-Michel Schönberg and Alain Boublil, the first being *Les Misérables.*

1990 He opens *Five Guys Named Moe* in the West End.

1990 Cameron inaugurates The Cameron Mackintosh Chair of Contemporary Theatre at Oxford University.

1990 Cameron is made an Honorary Fellow of St Catherine's College, Oxford.

1992 He is presented with the Richard Rodgers Award for Excellence in Musical Theatre.

1995 He produces the 10th anniversary performance of *Les Misérables* at the Royal Albert Hall.

1996 Cameron is knighted; he is now Sir Cameron Mackintosh.

1996 He opens the new Schönberg/Boublil musical *Martin Guerre* in the West End.

1998 A gala celebration, *Hey, Mr. Producer!* is held to mark Cameron's 30 years in the business. It is performed in the presence of Queen Elizabeth II and Prince Philip with proceeds going to the RNIB and the Combined Theatrical Charities.

1999 Cameron produces a revival of the musical *Oklahoma!*

2002 He receives the Oscar Hammerstein Award for Lifetime Achievement in Musical Theatre.

2002 He takes his revival of *Oklahoma!* to Broadway.

2004 After negotiating for years to secure the rights, Cameron finally opens *Mary Poppins* in the West End.

2006 He takes *Mary Poppins* to Broadway.

2006 His production of *Avenue Q* opens in the West End having transferred from Broadway.

2008 *Oliver!* opens in the West End.

OVERVIEW

Sir Cameron Mackintosh is currently one of the most successful theatre producers not only in Britain, but in the world, having presented productions both on tour and in the West End of London as well as on Broadway and throughout the world; he is also the owner of Delfont Mackintosh Theatres. From the time he saw *Salad Days*, all Sir Cameron wanted to do was produce his own shows and he achieved it with the likes of:

1960s

Anything Goes; Reluctant Debutante (The)

1970s

Card (The); Godspell; Lauder; My Fair Lady; Oklahoma!; Oliver!; Rock Nativity; Salad Days; Side by Side by Sondheim; Trelawny; Winnie the Pooh

15

1980s

Abbacadabra; Blondel; Boyfriend (The); Cats; Follies; Just So; Les Misérables; Little Shop of Horrors; Miss Saigon; Phantom of the Opera (The); Song and Dance; Tomfoolery

1990s

Card (The); Carousel; Five Guys Named Moe; Fix (The); Hey, Mr. Producer!; Martin Guerre; Moby Dick; Oklahoma!; Oliver!; Putting it Together

2000s

Avenue Q; Mary Poppins; My Fair Lady; Witches of Eastwick (The); Oliver!

Sir Trevor Nunn

1940 Trevor Robert Nunn is born on 14 January into a working-class family in Ipswich, England, son of Robert – a cabinet maker – and Dorothy May.

1951 He passes his Eleven Plus, which is his ticket to a grammar school education at Northgate Grammar School. In turn, this prepares him for a scholarship to Downing College, Cambridge where he throws himself into all things dramatic and becomes a member of the renowned Cambridge Footlights Club.

1953 Trevor starts his life on the stage when he begins acting with a local theatre company.

1957 He directs his own theatre group.

1964 Trevor joins the RSC.

1965 At not yet 25 years of age, he is made Associate Director of the RSC and so becomes the youngest person ever to hold this post. While there, he directs numerous classical dramas including the highly acclaimed – and eight-hour long – production of Charles Dickens' *Nicholas Nickleby*, which he directs with his colleague John Caird.

1969 Trevor marries Janet Suzman, with whom he has one child.

1981 He directs the musical *Cats* – which is all song and dance.

1985 Working once again with the director John Caird, he co-directs the musical *Les Misérables*, which is a co-production between The RSC and Cameron Mackintosh and which is set to make the RSC millions.

1986 Trevor and Janet divorce.

1986 He marries Sharon Lee Hill with whom he has two daughters.

1986 Trevor leaves the RSC.

1991 Trevor and Sharon divorce.

1994 Trevor marries actress Imogen Stubbs with whom he has two more children.

1996 He becomes Artistic Director of the National Theatre, London.

2002 Trevor is knighted by the Queen and becomes Sir Trevor Nunn.

2003 He retires from his position as Artistic Director at the National Theatre.

2004 In his usual futuristic, ground-breaking way, he introduces video projections into a traditional stage set production of Lloyd Webber's, *The Woman in White*.

2005 He directs Victoria Wood's musical comedy play, *Acorn Antiques*.

2008 Sir Trevor brings *Gone with the Wind*, to the West End stage – as a musical. It closes after two months.

OVERVIEW

Sir Trevor continues to work both in the subsidised and commercial theatre fields, in classical drama and musical theatre, and even in modern, musical comedy – as he did when he directed Victoria Wood's *Acorn Antiques*. It would appear that Sir Trevor Nunn does not concur with the suggestion that musical theatre is the poor relation of the thespian family! He is, without doubt, the epitome of theatrical intelligence and success. Just look at his catalogue of artistic successes:

MUSICALS (including musical plays)

Acorn Antiques; Arcadia; Around the World in Eighty Days; Aspects of Love; Baker's Wife (The); Blue Angel (The); Cats; Chess; Comedy of Errors (The); Gone with the Wind; Heartbreak House; Les Misérables; My Fair Lady; Oklahoma!; Royal Hunt of the Sun; South Pacific; Starlight Express; Sunset Boulevard; Woman in White (The)

OPERA

Così fan Tutte; Idomeneo; Katya Kabanova; Peter Grimes; Porgy and Bess; Sophie's Choice

STRAIGHT THEATRE

Albert Speer; Alchemist (The); All's Well That Ends Well; Amy's View; Antony and Cleopatra; Anything Goes; Arcadia; As You Like It; Betrayal; Blue Angel (The); Candide; Caucasion Chalk Circle; Cherry Orchard (The); Closer; Coast of Utopia (The); Comedy of Errors (The); Copenhagen;

Coriolanus; De Profundis; Enemy of the People; Every Good Boy Deserves Favour; Fair Maid of the West (The); Hamlet; Heartbreak House; Hedda Gabler; Henry IV Parts I & II; Henry V; Henry VIII; In Extremis; Julius Caesar; Juno and the Paycock, Othello; King Lear; Love's Labour's Lost; Macbeth; Measure for Measure; Merchant of Venice (The); Merry Wives of Windsor (The); Much Ado About Nothing; Mutabilitie; My Fair Lady; Nicholas Nickleby; Noises Off; Not About Nightingales; Once in a Lifetime; Othello; Peer Gynt; Peter Pan; Relapse (The); Relapse or Virtue in Danger (The); Revenger's Tragedy (The); Romeo and Juliet; Rose; Royal Hunt of the Sun (The); Salvage; Seagull (The); Shipwreck; South Pacific; Streetcar Named Desire (A); Summer Folk; Taming of the Shrew (The); Tango; Three Sisters; Thwarting of Baron Bolligrew (The); Timon of Athens; Titus Andronicus; Troilus and Cressida; View From a Bridge (A); Voyage; We Happy Few; Winter's Tale

TV

Antony and Cleopatra; Comedy of Errors (The); Every Good Boy Deserves Favour; Great Hamlets (The); Les Misérables in Concert; Life and Adventures of Nicholas Nickleby (The); Macbeth; Merchant of Venice (The); Oklahoma!; Othello; Porgy and Bess; Shakespeare Workshops Word of Mouth; Three Sisters (The)

Films

Hedda; Lady Jane; Twelfth Night

Chapter Two

The History of Musical Theatre

IKE everything else in this world, musical theatre has evolved, changed and developed over a vast period of time, influenced by the social and economic standards of any given period. Here, we will take a brief look at the past, which has shaped this very special art form right up until the present day, where it continues to grow and develop.

The Ancient Greeks

Contrary to popular belief, Andrew Lloyd Webber did not invent musical theatre, so the question is: Who did and more, to the point, when? In the words of Tim Rice from the musical *Joseph*, we need to go 'Way way back many centuries ago' to find the answer to that question. The ancient Greeks and the ancient Romans both had plays with music, but, sadly, the music itself has been lost to us and so we cannot say in all truth that their work influenced today's musical theatre (simply because we haven't actually heard it). But what we can say is that we were performing plays with music long ago, suggesting an inborn desire in us to sing and dance our way through a land of make believe.

Middle Ages

In this era, we come across travelling minstrels and we witness musical morality plays, known as Mystery Plays, staged by the churches. Some would have us believe that these had little to do with current trends, but I disagree. They were 'travelling minstrels', perhaps the precursor to cabaret artists on the club circuit (a way in which some of our present day artists begin their fledgling careers even today). We could similarly draw a comparison between them and the touring companies, which are very much a part of the modern thespian world. It is clear that our ways do have their roots in the traditions of past generations – even as far back as the Middle Ages. In fact, in the city of York, Mystery Plays are still being staged every four years and are a great tourist attraction. In addition to

the actual mystery plays themselves, spectacular bands of
touring actors travel the streets in
a wagon entertaining the locals
and tourists alike. So the
minstrels and morality plays
have travelled on and through to
our time, becoming a part of
our theatrical life.

York Mystery Plays

The Eighteenth and Nineteenth Centuries

I do not suggest that the Eighteenth Century gave us fully grown musical theatre, nor even musical theatre in its infancy, but I do suggest that it is here that we witnessed the formation of the foetus of musical theatre.

Strangely, in the Eighteenth and Nineteenth Centuries, we find there was a theatrical social status within theatre, not only in the UK but also in France and Germany, the other two strongholds of musical theatre. (At this point, it is worth mentioning how things have changed since then, for now it is the UK and the USA who are the strongholds of musical theatre, with Germany only really entering the 'family' quite recently and France seemingly disinterested in joining at all). This theatrical social status meant that theatre was more or less divided into two halves:

LOW COMEDIES

These were shows that were generally made up of 'borrowed' tunes with new lyrics written especially for them. The best known example of this kind of show in the English language theatre is John Gay's *The Beggar's Opera* (1728), which tells the tale of thieves and debauchery. This particular show 'borrowed' popular melodies such as 'Over the Hills and Far Away' as well as 'borrowing' from such composers as Purcell and Handel.

HIGH COMEDIES

These works, unlike the low comedies, boasted original music and usually more substantial plotlines. Although the music was more akin to grand opera, the stories were light-hearted as in Michael Balfe's *The Bohemian Girl* (1845), which tells the story of a nobleman's daughter who was raised by gypsies.

A more in-depth look at this period is not what this book is all about; I hope only to give you a taster from which, with whetted appetite, you can devour more from more relevant books if you should so wish. I therefore make no apology for moving swiftly on to the names of the Strauss family, with which most will be familiar, for we must not overlook the wonderful melodies they created and, as a consequence, their contribution to musical theatre as an art form and as a whole. The most famous member of this family was of course Johann Strauss II.

Johann Strauss II

Johann II was born on 25 October, 1825 and died on 3 June, 1899. He developed the popular, classical Viennese Waltzes, which enthralled not only his native Vienna but all of Europe and America for more than half a century. He also completed 16 works for the stage with *Die Fledermaus* (1874) and *The Gypsy Baron* (1885) being the most popular; the most famous of his waltzes was the much loved 'The Blue Danube' (1867). The music of Strauss was melodic and popular with the masses, and is generally recognised as being the root for the popular form of musical theatre which was to follow almost 100 years later.

Meanwhile, Britain in the 1800s saw the emergence of the music halls where theatres and bars combined to entertain the masses. These establishments thrived in their hundreds around the country, such was their popularity. The performers were often very mediocre, but in a form of theatre where the audience sang along, this slight flaw often went unnoticed! The shows themselves were a little risqué, though not offensively so. The British really took this sociable form of theatre to their hearts, so much so that the BBC broadcast a television programme entitled *The Good Old Days* from one of the few remaining music halls in the UK, the City Varieties Music Hall in Leeds, for 30 years from 1953–1983. Audiences attending the filming of this television show were traditionally asked to wear Victorian dress for the recording, which was so popular that, at one point, there were over 20,000 names on a list waiting for a ticket.

Gilbert and Sullivan

The next major milestone in musical theatre was the emergence of genius in the form of Messrs William S. Gilbert and Arthur S. Sullivan; this was an artistic marriage made in heaven and was probably one of the first of many such marriages to emerge over the next hundred years or more, the others being: George and Ira Gershwin, Rodgers and Hammerstein, Lerner and Loewe, Kander and Ebb, Lloyd Webber and Rice, Boublil and Schönberg.

There are cornerstones in musical theatre, pillars of excellence which support the past and contribute to the advancement of the future of this fine art. The pure genius of William S. Gilbert and Arthur S. Sullivan formed one of those cornerstones, which drew in millions of fans and admirers.

Gilbert and Sullivan – often referred to as G&S – produced works that were witty and melodic, a formula that was fast emerging as the key to theatrical success and, indeed, still is today. Starting with a commissioned piece, *Thespis*, the two went on to write a total of 14 light operas and were the first writers to produce the modern blockbuster musical. G&S works are still performed regularly today by both professional and amateur groups alike, such was and is their popularity. Indeed, the popularity of Gilbert and Sullivan operettas has now cast its magic across three centuries and continues to delight audiences to this day.

William Schwenk Gilbert

We know very little about Gilbert's relationship with his parents and little about Gilbert himself, except that he seemed to be a fiery individual. His abilities reached out in many directions.

We could be forgiven for believing that Gilbert was just one half of the G&S team; he was, in fact, so much more. He was a playwright – writing farces, operetta libretti, adapting novels and even venturing into French

W.S. Gilbert
Born: 18 November 1836
Died: 29 May 1911

translations – he was also an illustrator, a director, a set designer, a costume designer; he was an artist in every sense of the word but had another career as well, becoming a barrister and being called to the Bar at just 28.

WILLIAM GILBERT'S LIFE PRE-SULLIVAN

1836   Gilbert is born in London, the son of William Gilbert (a retired naval surgeon) and Anne Gilbert. He was the eldest of four children and had three younger sisters.

1849   (approx) Gilbert attends Ealing School; he completes his education at Kings College, London.

1857   Gilbert begins work as a government clerk and barrister, which does not work out for him.

1861   Gilbert contributes to a new magazine called *FUN* using the pen name Bab.

1860s During this decade, Gilbert begins his work as a dramatist – he will become prolific. He also studies the art of direction, an excellent tool for a serious dramatist – the route Gilbert is travelling along with great speed.

1867   Gilbert marries Lucy Agnes Turner.

1869   A collection of Gilbert's 'Babs Ballads' is published.

**It is now the end of Gilbert's life as a 'soloist'
and he becomes one half of the G&S partnership.**

Arthur Seymour Sullivan

It would seem that Arthur was not in possession of the same fiery nature as his partner, William Gilbert. Born into a musical family, he displayed his enormous talents at a very early age and later became the first Principal of the Royal College of Music, then known as the National Training School for Music. He was a prolific writer of music – including music for the stage – long before his partnership with Gilbert.

In 1875, the young impresario Richard D'Oyly Carte suggested to Gilbert that he ask Sullivan to write the music for a libretto he had completed – *Trial by Jury*.

Sullivan was often called upon to compose music for Royal State occasions.

A.S. Sullivan
Born: 13 May 1842
Died:
22 November 1900

ARTHUR SULLIVAN'S LIFE PRE-GILBERT

1842   Arthur Seymour Sullivan is born into a musical family – his father is a theatre musician and bandmaster, which means that, by the age of eight years, Arthur Sullivan can actually play every instrument in the military band.

1855   His first musical composition, *O Israel,* is published.

1856   Sullivan wins the competition for the first Mendelssohn Scholarship, meaning he is able to study at the Royal Academy of Music.

1858   Sullivan continues his musical studies at the prestigious Conservatory in Leipzig.

1862   His composition of incidental music to Shakespeare's *The Tempest* is given a highly successful public performance.

1860s   During this time, Sullivan becomes a prolific composer of mainly
–70s   serious and sacred work; he also becomes the first Principal of the Royal College of Music.

The Gilbert and Sullivan Partnership begins
and for those still in doubt:
Gilbert – words.
Sullivan – music.

1871   Gilbert and Sullivan collaborate on *Thespis* for John Hollingshead's Gaiety Theatre; sadly, it was unsuccessful. However, it was this piece that heralded the start of a very successful writing partnership that was to last for 25 years.

1871   During the year that *Thespis* did not achieve artistic acclaim, Gilbert writes two other plays, which are at least financially rewarding.

1875   Richard D'Oyly Carte commissions Gilbert and Sullivan to write a short piece for the Royalty Theatre, which he is managing at the time. The piece is *Trial by Jury* and the result is the start of a tri-partnership which is destined to bring unprecedented fame to all three.

1877   Richard commissions another piece from the pair – *The Sorcerer.* More are to follow, almost annually.

1879   Richard D'Oyly Carte, in a clever business move, obtains the rights to be the sole producer of Gilbert and Sullivan's works, including the rights to all amateur productions and band parts. There followed with almost alarming speed:

1878	*H.M.S. Pinafore*
1879	*The Pirates of Penzance*
1881	*Patience*
1882	*Iolanthe*
1884	*Princess Ida*
1885	*The Mikado*
1887	*Ruddigore*
1888	*The Yeoman of the Guard*
1889	*The Gondoliers*

**The collaboration of Gilbert and Sullivan made them both
very wealthy men, but it made Richard D'Oyly Carte
even wealthier!**

1881 Richard D'Oyly Carte builds the Savoy Theatre for the purpose of producing Gilbert and Sullivan works; he then builds the Savoy Hotel.

1883 Sullivan is knighted for his services to music.

1890 'The carpet quarrel': Gilbert writes to Sullivan saying that the time has come to end their collaboration, ostensibly the reason being an argument over a new carpet at the Savoy Theatre. In reality, however, the quarrel goes much deeper.

1900 Sullivan dies on 22 November – the feast day of St Cecilia, the patron saint of music.

1907 Gilbert is knighted.

1911 Gilbert dies while trying to save a woman from drowning.

OVERVIEW

Gilbert and Sullivan were two enormously intelligent and talented men. It is fair to say that, had they been a man and woman, they would possibly never have married – not successfully anyway – for they both had so much to give that they were bound to clash. However, they did have an artistic marriage.

We know that a good marriage is generally a series of compromises and compromising artistically is often far more difficult than compromising within a marriage. And don't forget, in this 'marriage' there was also a third person – Richard D'Oyly Carte – which of course always spells disaster!

Gilbert, as I have said, was a fiery individual who was used to getting his own way, but in terms of the G&S partnership, he was only one half of it, with only one half of the say – and only one third of the say when Richard D'Oyly Carte's input was taken into consideration. But partnerships always become unbalanced when one partner is temperamentally more caustic than the other(s), as was the case with Gilbert. He was also very hands-on with directing, costume and sets and the lead in deciding the 'feel' of whatever piece the pair were writing; thus Sullivan felt that the works were plays with a few songs and so the 50:50 slant never really rang true in Sullivan's eyes – add to that the third party in the presence of the producer Richard D'Oyly Carte and the balance is knocked further out of kilter. Gilbert wanted a finger in every pie and checked the finances very carefully, which led to him accusing Richard of being responsible for the unnecessary expense of a new carpet for the Savoy (the carpet quarrel). Like all arguments have a tendency to do, this argument escalated out of control and, as the pair were not really getting on, Sullivan was hardly likely to take Gilbert's side in the carpet quarrel; so this, historically and conveniently, has been blamed for the break up of the artistically and financially lucrative tri-partnership. Later, unsuccessful, attempts were made to work together, but old wounds rarely heal.

The Works of Gilbert and Sullivan

We must never forget that both Gilbert and Sullivan had successful careers independently of each other. However, during the productive years when working with Richard D'Oyly Carte, they wrote and produced some of the most enduring operettas of all time. Below is a short synopsis of their best known works.

H.M.S. PINAFORE (1878)

OUTLINE PLOT
This is the story of love between members of different social classes. Take the Captain of a ship and his daughter, who has fallen in love with a common sailor, who also happens to be serving on her father's ship and you're heading for trouble – especially when said Captain has arranged for his daughter to marry the First Lord of the Admiralty, a sailor who has never actually been to sea! Then there is the fact that the Captain himself fancies a poor bum-boat woman. Complicated? Yes, but despite the complications, it all works out happily ever after!

HMS *Pinafore*

NOTES

Poor Mr Sullivan was criticised for this piece as many did not think his music matched the standard of the libretto. One wonders whether this caused an argument between the tempestuous two, or whether, behind closed doors, Gilbert came out in support of Sullivan . . . if only walls had tongues as well as ears!

THE PIRATES OF PENZANCE (1879)

OUTLINE PLOT

Frederic is a young apprentice pirate who has come to the end of his term of apprenticeship, which it turns out was a mistake anyway, being the result of his half-deaf nurse mistaking the word pirate for pilot; he was, in fact, supposed to be an apprentice 'pilot'!

He decides to leave the pirates but, before he does, he points out the reason why they are not very successful pirates is because they are too soft-hearted. It transpires that anyone captured by them who then professes to be an orphan is immediately released.

Up until this point, Frederic has never seen a woman other than his old

nurse – who has mistakenly led him to believe that she is beautiful, which she most certainly is not! Once on shore, he meets up with a group of truly beautiful women and falls in love with one of them. The pirates then capture all of the women, who are subsequently released when their father arrives and pleads that he is an orphan!

Add to this the fact that Frederic, who was born on 29 February, has only had a birthday every four years, and is therefore deemed not to have served his full apprenticeship – which as a 'good' man he insists on doing – and you have the usual array of ridiculous situations and people; you also have the usual G&S hit and the happy ever after ending!

Notes

The first performance of *The Pirates of Penzance* was on 30 December, 1879 in Paignton, England. It was, though, just one performance and was for copyright purposes only. The true première was actually the following day, 31 December, in New York at the Fifth Avenue Theatre. The first London performance was not until 3 April, 1880 at the Opéra Comique.

PATIENCE (1881)

OUTLINE PLOT

It is an era in which aestheticism rules except, that is, in the life of a simple milkmaid by the name of Patience. All the young ladies in the village are in love with two poets; the poets however, are only in love with Patience. Even the soldiers turn to poetry in the hope that it will win them a lady. Of course, all eventually win the right person as one would expect in a G&S operetta.

NOTES

This was a very topical piece at a time when the craze for poets, or anyone with any aesthetic leanings at all, was at its height. For this reason, some feel that it makes *Patience* more inaccessible now. I fail to see why, as all G&S plots were so outrageous that another peculiarity hardly matters at all!

IOLANTHE (1882)

OUTLINE PLOT

This is the fairy story of Strephon, an Arcadian shepherd who is half fairy – his upper half being fairy, his legs being mortal – and who wants to marry Phyllis. Phyllis, however, does not know that Strephon is half fairy and so, when she sees him kissing a young woman, she assumes the worst. What she does not know is that the 'young' woman in question is actually Strephon's own mother, who is also a fairy – and, of course, fairies

never grow old so how could she be expected to know when his mother looked so young!

Things are further complicated by the fact that Phyllis' guardian, the Lord Chancellor and half the Peers in the House of Lords have designs on her too, the result being that, very soon, the Peers and the fairies are virtually at war – but, of course, all ends happily ever after; wel,l it is G&S after all.

NOTES

This is one of the least appreciated of the G&S stable and yet there are so many interesting interwoven tales that one often wonders why. This was also payback time for Mr Sullivan after the criticisms aimed at him after *H.M.S. Pinafore*. This time, the critics preferred his music to Gilbert's lyrics!

On the opening night, the audience of *Iolanthe* were each given a copy of the libretto, however, the result was that they were so preoccupied with reading it that they barely looked at the stage! Was this the reason the critics preferred the music? We'll never know.

And when you next write your Christmas shopping list, murmur a quiet thank you to Messrs G&S as you add the words 'fairy lights', for this term was born of the small lights that the principal fairies wore on top of their heads, which were operated by a small battery placed on their shoulders and hidden by their long hair.

THE MIKADO (1885)

OUTLINE PLOT

Nanki-Poo, the son of the Mikado of Japan, has fled his father's court in order to escape marriage to Katisha, an elderly, ugly lady. In order to escape, he disguised himself as a wandering minstrel and it was at this time that he met and fell in love with Yum-Yum, the young ward of Ko-Ko, a tailor in the town of Titipu. Yum-Yum, however, was already betrothed to her guardian and so was not free to love Nanki-Poo who, as a consequence, left Titipu in despair. He later returns on hearing that Ko-Ko has been condemned to death for flirting, believing that he might be able to claim Yum-Yum's love.

But this is a G&S operetta and so nothing is that straightforward. We have the complications of a man who is all things to all people, and the possibility of a self-decapitation; but then, because it *is* a G&S operetta, everything turns out well and everyone lives happily ever after – and with heads intact!

NOTES

The *Mikado* is probably the most well-loved of all G&S works, and often affectionately referred to as *Mick-a-doo* proving yet again that a nickname is the most tangible form of recognition and affection. This delightful work came about partly by accident – or fate for those who believe in such things.

After *Princess Ida*, Gilbert was casting his creative eye beyond the British shores for his next piece of inspiration when, one day, an

unexpected accident inspired him with an idea. An old Japanese sword which for years had been hanging on the wall of his study suddenly, and without warning, fell from its place; and so there it was on the floor, the inspiration for the next G&S operetta, *The Mikado*.

THE YEOMAN OF THE GUARD (1888)

OUTLINE PLOT

Colonel Fairfax is to be beheaded in an hour's time on a false charge of sorcery. He has no wish to leave his estate to his cousin (who is also his accuser) and, to avoid this, he secretly marries a strolling singer by the name of Elsie Maynard, who agrees because, after his death, she expects to become a wealthy widow – and a widow, of course, is what she expects to be in just an hour's time. She is conventiently blindfolded for the ceremony and so never actually gets to see Colonel Fairfax, the man she is marrying.

However, before he can be beheaded, disguised as a Yeoman of the Guard, Fairfax escapes and guess what? He meets and falls in love for real with Elsie! She falls in love with him too, not realising that she is actually falling in love with her own 'husband'; how could she for she was blind-folded when she married him. She had previously been loved by Jack Point, but she leaves him a broken man in favour of Fairfax.

THE YEOMEN OF THE GUARD

NOTES

Many think that this is Sullivan's finest score. It is certainly the darkest of the operettas and all do not live happily ever after as in most of their works.

THE GONDOLIERS (1889)

OUTLINE PLOT

This is the story of two Venetian gondoliers who, having just got married, are informed that one of them has just become the King of Barataria. No one knows which of the two it is, but to further complicate things, whoever it is was, in fact, married in infancy to Casilda, daughter of the Duke of Plaza-Torobut. It is the usual series of G&S confused identities, followed by a happy ending.

NOTES

This is the 12th operetta by the pair and the last to achieve worldwide acclaim. What sets this apart from the previous works is that, compared to their other operettas, this one required far more dancing.

The Twentieth Century

This light opera form of 'musical theatre' flourished well into the Twentieth Century, carried on the back of the talents of the likes of Franz Lehar, who composed the music for *The Merry Widow* (1907), Rudolph Friml who composed the music for *Rose Marie* (1924) and *The Vagabond King* (1925) and Sigmund Romberg's *The Student Prince* (1924) and *The Desert Song* (1926).

WHAT ELSE WAS HAPPENING AS WE ENTER THE TWENTIETH CENTURY?

Pantomime:

This is a very special form of theatre – indeed musical theatre – which has survived across the centuries and right up to this very day when it has become a British institution. Some of the most popular pantomimes today are: *Cinderella, Snow White, Sleeping Beauty, Aladdin, Babes in the Wood* and *Dick Whittington*. These shows involve the retelling of well known fairy tales and usually involve men dressed as women (Dames), and women dressed as men (Principal Boys). Then there are the dancing cows and agile cats, as well as all things magical from lamps to apples and beans to mice. Add to this heightened audience participation and you a have a show that can only be called 'unique'.

Minstrel Shows:

Minstrel shows started in the mid-Nineteenth Century and continued to be a popular form of entertainment up to the mid-Twentieth Century – in the UK up until the 1970s when the BBC continued to show *The Black and White Minstrel Show*. As the UK became increasingly multi-racial and multi-cultural, these shows became unacceptable forms of entertainment.

The Music Halls:

The music halls, which started in the Nineteenth Century, continued to thrive into and on through the Twentieth Century where they became home to variety performers and where a stage and a bar were of equal importance! At first, they catered mainly for the working classes with their bawdy style of humour and free-flowing alcohol, but later enticed in folks from all walks of life. After the First World War, variety theatre took over, but the old musical halls refused to go away entirely. They still exist to this day, primarily in the north of England where they are now Working Mens' Clubs. Many young singers, and comedians too, have started their professional lives in these clubs, and they do say that if you can survive a critical Working Mens' Club audience, you can survive any audience.

Vaudeville:

While the music halls were digging the foundations for the future of modern musical theatre in the UK, in the US, the same can be said of Vaudeville shows. They were very similar in format to the British music halls in that, although they presented a variety of acts, the accent was firmly on song and dance.

The foundations for future musicals had been laid and everything was in place for musical theatre to really take off in a huge commercial way. It was now time for the advent of US and UK domination, some would say competition. Musical theatre mania was about to begin!

America gives the world Cole Porter, Rodgers and Hart, later Rodgers and Hammerstein, the Gershwins and many, many more composers and lyricists as the Twentieth Century progresses on, and into, the Twenty-first Century.

It is no different on the other side of the Atlantic with the British first presenting the flamboyant Noel Coward and Ivor Novello to the world of musical theatre and then going on to produce such outstanding talents as Lionel Bart, Andrew Lloyd Webber, Tim Rice and Leslie Bricusse.

And so the race is on with the American musical versus the British – the winner is both, because both nations are virtually unrivalled. However, they better beware because the French have proved that they can produce amazing talent such as Alain Boublil and Claude-Michel Schönberg, and the Germans have proved that they can mount spectacular productions of successful musicals such as *We Will Rock You*, which many argue is superior to the British production and, in fact, quite the best of all the worldwide productions of this musical.

The Twentieth Century is the start of the Musical Theatre Revolution as it seems that the whole world now loves a musical.

From the 1920s to the present day, the world, and in particular the US and the UK, has feasted on an abundance of gourmet musicals, both on the stage and on the screen with no sign of a famine in sight; on the contrary, each decade sees yet more musicals produced and appetites growing as we demand ever more.

Musical Milestones

Up until 1920, it seemed that the growth of musical theatre had followed a fairly gentle and predictable path of progress but, after 1920, it forged forward at an almost alarming speed, mirroring the equally fast changing world and world events which were set to shape and change our future in a way which no one could ever have predicted.

The social and economic state of the world has always played a great part in the entertainment industry, having a direct influence upon, and been reflected in, the 'story-telling world' of theatre and film. And so it was that these unforgettable social milestones of the Twentieth and early Twenty-first Century led and pointed the way to those who were travelling the path of entertainment taking us to the point at which we now find ourselves – where musicals dominate both Broadway and the West End and where the study of this art form is even recognised in Higher Education.

When looking at the growth of musical theatre, it is always fascinating to take a glimpse at what is happening in the 'real' world too, for theatre, whether musical or otherwise, does not and cannot exist in isolation, but is a part of the bigger picture; and a reflection of the bigger picture too, be it consciously or subconsciously.

THE GROWTH OF MUSICAL THEATRE

1920s

During this decade, women were given the right to equal votes with men in both the UK and America • Prohibition began in America • the Oxford Dictionary was finally finished • penicillin was discovered • Einstein's General Theory of Relativity was created • Walt Disney arrived in Hollywood and the Mickey Mouse cartoons began • Wall Street crashed in 1929

This was the decade of liberation for, until this point, there were both social and economic constraints placed upon women; men considered themselves to be the superior sex. The First World War had ended and, with it, many of the shackles borne by women were discarded too. In 1918, they were even allowed to vote, but only if they were over the age of 30 and were householders or the wives of householders. Fashions were more liberal too and being an entertainer was (more or less) acceptable. It is interesting to note, though, that women's fashion had a masculine feel; that is straight up and down and with nothing to indicate a curvy figure beneath. Even women's hairstyles were short and masculine at this time. It was almost a subconscious public declaration indicating that men were still considered superior.

The notable musicals to open during this decade were: *No, No, Nanette* (1925) and *The Vagabond King* (1925), which went on to transfer to the West End in 1927. Although *The Vagabond King* initially had a longer run than *No, No, Nanette*, it is the latter that has actually proven to be the more enduring of the two musicals. Then, of course, there was *Lady be Good* (1924), which heralded stardom for the 'song and dance man' Fred Astaire. After that, came the forward-thinking musical *Show Boat* (1927), by composer Jerome Kern and librettist/lyricist Oscar Hammerstein II, which broke down social boundaries by dealing with the problem of racism, unthinkable until that time. It is a musical which publicly points out the wrongs of colour prejudice, musical theatre making a tangible contribution to the world of politics.

1930s

Following the Wall Street Crash, the world was in an economic black hole • polythene was discovered • driving tests began in the UK • King George V died • King Edward VIII abdicated • his brother became King George VI • 999 emergency calls began in London • The Golden Gate Bridge opened in San Francisco • Lajos Biro produced the ballpoint pen • Britain declared war on Germany

This was the decade of depression, except in the world of musical theatre where it was in fact the decade of romantic escapism! In the 1930s, the world was suffering an economic Depression. In addition, alcohol (which had been banned in America since the 1920s Prohibition) would continue to be prohibited until 1933 and, in the UK, the lack of work in the North-East led to the protest march known as the Jarrow Hunger March. So, what did the 'ordinary' man in the street do when faced with all this misery? He tried to escape and imagine himself as part of a happier life! He went to the theatre or to the cinema to watch romantic comedies and listen to beautiful music; he romanticised about his own dreary life. It is interesting to note that *Porgy and Bess*, by George and Ira Gershwin, was not the success it later became when it first opened in 1935. Perhaps this was because it depicted everything from which the man in the street was trying to escape.

Rodgers and Hart wrote some wonderful escapist musicals at this time, which served as a haven for the troubled and impoverished. These included: *On Your Toes* (1936), *Babes in Arms* (1937), *I'd Rather be Right* (1937), *I Married an Angel* (1938), *The Boys From Syracuse* (1938), *Too Many Girls* (1939).

But the writer who really provided an escape route for the depressed millions was Cole Porter, and the reason for this was that he himself came from money and had money; he had experienced the life that most could only dream about and perhaps, as a result of this, he had more hits in this decade than any other writer. He composed the scores for many musical films as well as numerous stage musicals such as: *Gay Divorce* (1932) and *Anything Goes* (1934).

Me and My Girl (1937) with music by Noel Gay, book and lyrics by Arthur Rose and Douglas Furber, was the escapist rags to riches musical which dominated the London scene. However, with its Cockney leanings – on a lamppost! – it was not thought to be suitable for transfer across the pond and in fact took almost 50 years to set sail; when it did, the Americans loved it!

And then, just when no one thought it could get any worse . . .

1939 The Second World War began

1940s

Nylon stockings went on sale in America • Japan attacked Pearl Harbor • America entered the Second World War • antibiotics came into use • Hitler committed suicide (1945) • two atomic bombs were dropped on Japan • the end of the Second World War (1945) • National Health Services started in the UK in 1948 • apartheid started in South Africa

This was the decade of patriotism as the world was at war for 50 per cent of it, and everyone, in all countries, felt in patriotic mood; in Britain, patriotic songs abounded such as: 'The White Cliffs of Dover' and 'We'll Meet Again', but it was to the theatre and to the cinema that the afraid and troubled went once again to block out what was going on around them. And so the new musicals continued in the escapist mode of the 1930s, although there was a very obvious attempt to make musical theatre grow up and progress beyond the trivial; and so it was that messages were creeping into the plots. But more importantly, Rodgers and Hammerstein were proving that a musical was more than a coat hanger for songs. They led the way in showing the next generation that to have a successful musical you *must* have a sound storyline; as a result they gave us *Oklahoma!* (1943). Now true musical theatre had really begun where every element, be it melody, lyrics, choreography or set, had the same purpose and that was to drive the story forward. Equally important at this globally fragile time was that each tale had a moral, and that good triumphed over bad. People needed hope and trust. They needed to believe that their world was not all bad. Depth of plot and characterisation had arrived and two dimensional plots and characters had no further place in this new world of musical theatre.

Where Rodgers and Hammerstein led, others followed and the musical was reaching maturity. New writers emerged from the shadows giving us great storylines in the musicals of Burton Lane and E.Y. Harburg's *Finian's Rainbow* (1947) and Lerner and Loewe's *Brigadoon* (1947).

The decade drew to a close with another Rodgers and Hammerstein great, *South Pacific* (1949). It is said that this is the musical inspiration behind Lloyd Webber, which is hardly surprising as the score is beautiful, the storyline touches the public conscience, there are not one but two love stories and dance for dance's sake has gone.

1950s

King George VI died and his eldest daughter became Queen Elizabeth II • Eisenhower became President of the US • The Mousetrap opened in London • the contraceptive pill was created • sweet rationing came to an end (1953) • Hillary and Tensing conquered Everest • the vaccine against polio was developed • Roger Bannister ran the four minute mile • Bill Haley and the Comets released 'Rock around the Clock' • the first comprehensive school opened in London • CND was formed • the Queen's first Christmas broadcast (1957) • The Beatles were formed • Buddy Holly was killed in a plane crash • the Mini car was launched • first section of the M1 opened in Britain

To those who had survived the war, this was their decade; the decade of youth. And for the young who had never been called to fight, they were simply delighted that the threat had gone away and they could now relax and enjoy their lives. In the UK, the Americans had left behind not only nylon stockings but a legacy of new and exciting music. The Americans and their culture was our new best friend and we were to become ever more permanently artistically entwined.

Many theatre goers call the 1950s the Golden Decade of musical theatre and, in this theatrical mountain range, stand three great peaks. One is a musical monster for any musician and yet ask any musician what is the greatest musicals score ever written and 90 per cent will reply *West Side Story* (1957); another has been seen by almost everyone. I am, of course, referring to *The Sound of Music* (1959); and the third, *My Fair Lady* (1956), is, quite simply, a masterpiece of theatrical crafting which satisfies even the literary doubters. Add to this *Guys and Dolls* (1950), *Gypsy* (1959) and *The King and I* (1951) and you can see why it is seen as the Golden Decade of musical theatre.

1960s

*MOT tests were introduced • John F. Kennedy became President of the US
(1961) • the Berlin wall was built • Cuban Missile Crisis (1962) brought
the world to the brink of nuclear war • thalidomide was withdrawn • John
Glenn became the first American in orbit • Britain froze in the winter of
ice (1963) • first raids on Vietnam by the USA (1965) • Winston Churchill
died (1965) • TV cigarette commercials banned in Britain • death penalty
abolished in Britain • England won the World Cup • Aberfan disaster
killed 144 (116 were children) • Six Day War in Middle East closed the
Suez Canal for eight years • colour TV seen in Britain • Che Guevara
(Evita) killed in Bolivia • first human heart transplant • Enoch Powell
delivered his 'Rivers of Blood Speech' • John F. Kennedy was assassinated
(1963) • Robert F. Kennedy (John's brother) was murdered (1968) • last
steam passenger train ran in Britain • Martin Luther King was assassinated (1968) • the Irish 'problem' erupted • man first landed on the moon
(Neil Armstrong and Buzz Aldrin)*

If the 1950s was the decade of youth then the 1960s was a double helping
of it. Some of the young of this decade believed that the way to fight a
war was with peace, hence the saying: 'Make Love Not War', and their
weapons were flowers: 'Flower Power'.

Having made great musical strides in the 1950s, the 1960s seemed to
be a time when creativity slowed down a little to an 'amble along' stage.
There were some excellent musicals in this era such as *Fiddler On the
Roof* (1964) and *Half a Sixpence* (1963), but little of ground-breaking
importance other than *Joseph and the Amazing Technicolor Dreamcoat*
(1968), which launched the phenomenal careers of Andrew Lloyd Webber
and Tim Rice and which was billed as a rock opera. (I doubt it would be
billed as such today, not because it doesn't deserve such a title but
because it would probably be considered 'too gentle'.) Then there was
Oliver! (1960), and what can possibly be said about *Oliver!* except that it
was destined to be a 'lifer', loved and cherished by future generations?

Until the 1950s, musical theatre and popular music were somewhat
intrinsically entwined in that one could expect to hear show tunes on the
radio which, of course, then sold the show. In the 1950s, the separation
process began and, by the 1960s, there was a whole new 'pop' music
scene. Songs from musicals and popular music were divorced from each
other; songs from the shows were no longer popular choices for radio
shows and musical theatre had to find a way ahead without the help of
the popular music scene. A by-product of this was that it was becoming

a genre in its own right like never before, which was of course good, but it did mean that there was a slowing down in the progress of musical theatre.

Towards the end of the 1960s was a musical which epitomised the era, *Hair* (1967). Ironically, it was so 'of its time' that it hasn't had the number of revivals one would expect of a musical of this calibre.

1970s

Decimalisation was introduced into the UK and the Republic of Ireland • Rolls Royce was declared bankrupt • Britain entered the EEC • ceasefire in Vietnam • first telephone call was made on a mobile phone • Charlie Chaplin was knighted • end of the Vietnam War • Yorkshire Ripper began his reign of terror • Microsoft arrived • National Theatre opened (1976) • Elvis died • world's first test-tube baby was born (Louise Brown) • Margaret Thatcher became the first female PM in the UK

So we limped into the 1970s with our art lost in a fog. Then along came Andrew Lloyd Webber and Tim Rice's *Jesus Christ Superstar* (1971), which first opened on Broadway; little did anyone know at the time that this musical was to set a precedent for future generations. It was a rock opera where dialogue was set to music and would lead the way for a new generation of writers. Musical theatre was up and away again, this time at breakneck speed. Soon, it would be realised that nothing was going to stop it.

Grease (1972) arrived to become one of the most enduring musicals of all time, but sadly it also became one of the most massacred musicals of all time, as everyone believes they can 'do' Grease and therefore they do not approach it with any respect or thought but merely throw it onto the stage believing that energy alone will carry it through – which it will not.

This was the decade of rebellion – a breakneck decade; the young had become more vocal in their demands and expected more from life than previous generations. Whereas the lives of their forefathers had been blighted by war, this was no longer the case for the new generation. Yes, there were wars, but not on the same global scale; there was less one-to-one combat, resulting in the loss of fewer lives. The young, to a certain extent, ruled the world and let everyone know it. They went in all directions and experienced life as never before – something musical theatre reflected.

Children were entertained and encouraged into the theatre by *Annie* (1970) and we were shocked and thrilled by *The Rocky Horror Show*

(1973) and *Tommy* (1979). Lloyd Webber and Rice gave us *Evita* (1978); Fosse thrilled us with his unique form of dance in *Chicago* (1975) while Sondheim astounded us with the depth of his intellectual writing in *Sweeney Todd* (1979). Yes, in the 1970s musical theatre was racing in every direction, never pausing for breath but always progressing. Not only was the musical getting bigger and better in an artistic sense, but it was also costing more and more to mount. Investors were paying far more with their sights set on larger returns – but more to gain meant more to lose.

This section cannot possibly end without a mention of the musical which for some *is* Broadway, namely *A Chorus Line* (1975), which opened on Broadway in 1975, not closing until 1990.

1980s

John Lennon was murdered in New York • first case of Aids in the USA • Prince Charles and Lady Diana Spencer married • Argentina invaded the Falklands • Princes William and Harry were born • first artificial heart in America • York Minster struck by lightening • IRA bomb exploded at Tory conference hotel in Brighton • Live Aid raised over £50 million • wreck of the Titanic discovered • Chernobyl nuclear accident • M25 completed • Berlin Wall brought down (1989)

This was the decade in which musical theatre came of age and produced some of the most diverse and enduring classics, which is rather strange considering that, as a decade it was rather bland, teetering as it was on the edge of a technological revolution.

At the start of this decade, many homes still didn't have video recorders and the CD player was not yet in mass production; to own the 'new fangled' mobile phone meant spending hours in the gym just to build up the strength to carry the monster around!

It was also the decade in which the musical game of Broadway v. the West End was won by the West End – or so say some. Bigger and more successful musicals were coming out of the West End than off Broadway, however, in my opinion there can be no winner in a game where there are no rules. And, as far as I am aware, no one has written a rule book on what the public can enjoy. Each of us should be allowed to enjoy a musical for whatever reason we choose.

The 1980s gave us the spectacular musicals of *Cats* (1980) and the roller-skating spectacular, *Starlight Express* (1984), both with music by Andrew Lloyd Webber. The excitement of these two musicals enticed a young and new generation of theatre goers into the theatre. *The Little Shop of Horrors*

(1982) and *Bugsy Malone* (1983) brought us humour. Homage was paid to classical literature through *Les Misérables* (1985), *The Phantom of the Opera* (1986) and *Return to the Forbidden Planet* (1989). Stephen Sondheim's unique style was celebrated with *Into the Woods* (1986) and those who enjoyed the old-style musical were catered for by stage versions of *Seven Brides for Seven Brothers* (1982), *High Society* (1987), *Singin' in the Rain* (1983) and *42nd Street* (1980). And these musicals were only the tip of the iceberg. What a decade!

Another thing that this extraordinary decade brought to us was a look at the marketing aspect of theatre. This was the decade in which the poster and the merchandising became almost as big as the show itself. Marketing campaigns were planned with military precision and put into action long before the show hit the boards. Musical theatre was now big business.

1990s

Nelson Mandela released from prison in South Africa • Margaret Thatcher forced to resign as PM • Queen Elizabeth II became the first monarch in the UK to pay income tax • the National Lottery started • scientists cloned a sheep (Dolly) • Harry Potter arrived

This was the decade in which technology truly arrived and, as a consequence, opened up so many possibilities to so many; the world suddenly became both greater and smaller all at the same time.

For musical theatre, however, the momentum of the last decade slowed down considerably and a new era began; an era of corporate musicals in the form of Disney who brought us *Beauty and the Beast* (1994) and *The Lion King* (1997) and the start of catalogue musicals such as *Mamma Mia* (1999). Catalogue musicals were not exactly a new thing, but the phenomenal success of *Mamma Mia* gave them a new credibility and encouraged others to follow suit well into the next decade.

2000s

Concorde crashed • the US Twin Towers were attacked and destroyed by terrorists • 12 European countries adopted the Euro – but not Britain • the Queen Mother died (2002) • the congestion charge was introduced in London • England won the Rugby World Cup • Pope John Paul died; Pope Benedict XVI was elected • London heard that it was to host the 2012 Olympic Games • and was bombed the following day • smoking was banned in public places in the UK • Tony Blair steped down as PM to be replaced by Gordon Brown

There is no stopping progress, as the 'noughties' have shown us, and there is no stopping regression either, for this is the decade of contradictions. In modern society, most people have a mobile phone, but few know how to communicate and so violence escalates, we care to the point where compassion masks understanding and this sometimes hampers progress.

In the world of musical theatre, this is a decade of diversity and individuality where anything goes! There is less of what is 'right' and what is 'wrong' and more of individual freedom and artistic expression as we enjoy such musicals as *Acorn Antiques* (2005) – more of a play with music than a musical – and nostalgically take a trip into the past with *Spamalot* (2005) to remember Monty Python. We have *Avenue Q* (2003) – more than a little rude, but now acceptable – and *We Will Rock You* (2002) – a loud and exciting celebration of the music of Queen. Then comes *The Woman in White* (2004) – a musical version of Wilkie Collins' classic novel of the same name. So you see, there really is no pattern emerging as to what direction musical theatre will now take. But surely this doesn't matter, for it leaves the doors wide open for any artist to take it in any direction whatsoever. And that is good news!

Chapter Three

Looking for Information?

SOME say that intelligence can be measured not by taking an IQ test, but by how many questions one asks.

In this section, you will find the answers to questions I have been asked most frequently by my own students – and a few answers to questions they should be asking me!

A–Z of Popular Stage Musicals

Below is a list of just *some* of the musicals of the Twentieth and Twenty-first Centuries; the date tells us the year of the first *stage* production

MUSICAL	YEAR	MUSIC	LYRICS	BOOK
A				
Acorn Antiques	2005	Victoria Wood	Victoria Wood	Victoria Wood
Act (The)	1977	John Kander	Fred Ebb	George Furth
Aida	1998	Elton John	Tim Rice	Linda Woolverton Robert Falls David Henry Hwang
Allegro	1947	Richard Rodgers	Oscar Hammerstein II	Oscar Hammerstein II
Annie	1977	Charles Strouse	Martin Charnin	Thomas Meehan
Annie Get Your Gun	1946	Irving Berlin	Irving Berlin	Herbert & Dorothy Fields
Anyone Can Whistle	1964	Stephen Sondheim	Stephen Sondheim	Arthur Laurents
Anything Goes	1934	Cole Porter	Cole Porter	P.G. Wodehouse Howard Lindsay Russell Crouse Guy Bolton
Applause	1970	Charles Strouse	Lee Adams	Betty Comden Adolph Green
Aspects of Love	1989	Andrew Lloyd Webber	Don Black Charles Hart	Don Black Charles Hart
Assassins	1991	Stephen Sondheim	Stephen Sondheim	John Weidman

MUSICAL	YEAR	MUSIC	LYRICS	BOOK
Avenue Q	2003	Robert Lopez Jeff Marx	Robert Lopez Jeff Marx	Jeff Whitty

B

MUSICAL	YEAR	MUSIC	LYRICS	BOOK
Babes in Arms	1937	Richard Rodgers	Lorenz Hart	Richard Rodgers Lorenz Hart
Baby	1983	David Shire	Richard Maltby Jr	Sybille Pearson
Bad Girls – the Musical	2006	Kath Gotts	Kath Gotts	Maureen Chadwick Ann McManus
Baker's Wife (The)	1989	Stephen Schwartz	Stephen Schwartz	Joseph Stein
Barnum	1980	Cy Coleman	Michael Stewart	Mark Bramble
Bat Boy	2001	Laurence O'Keefe	Laurence O'Keefe	Keythe Farley Brian Flemming
Beautiful Game (The)	2000	Andrew Lloyd Webber	Ben Elton	Ben Elton
Beauty and the Beast	1994	Alan Menken	Howard Ashman Tim Rice	Linda Woolverton
Bells are Ringing (The)	1956	Jule Styne	Betty Comden Adolph Green	Betty Comden Adolph Green
Bernadette	1990	Gwyn Hughes	Maureen Hughes	Maureen Hughes
Best Little Whorehouse in Texas (The)	1978	Carol Hall	Carol Hall	Larry King Peter Masterson
Big River	1985	Roger Miller	Roger Miller	William Hauptman
Big the Musical	1996	David Shire	Richard Maltby Jr	John Weidman
Billy	1974	John Barry	Don Black	Dick Clement Ian La Frenais
Billy Elliot	2005	Elton John	Lee Hall	Lee Hall
Bitter Sweet	1929	Noel Coward	Noel Coward	Noel Coward
Bless the Bride	1947	Vivian Ellis	A.P. Herbert	A P. Herbert
Blitz	1962	Lionel Bart	Lionel Bart	Lionel Bart Joan Maitland
Blondel	1983	Stephen Oliver	Tim Rice	Tim Rice
Blood Brothers	1983	Willy Russell	Willy Russell	Willy Russell
Bombay Dreams	2002	A.R. Rahman	Don Black	Meera Syal
Bounce	2003	Stephen Sondheim	Stephen Sondheim	John Weidman
Boyfriend (The)	1954	Sandy Wilson	Sandy Wilson	Sandy Wilson
Boys From Syracuse (The)	1938	Richard Rodgers	Lorenz Hart	George Abbott
Brigadoon	1947	Frederick Loewe	Alan Jay Lerner	Alan Jay Lerner

MUSICAL	YEAR	MUSIC	LYRICS	BOOK
Buddy	1989	Based on the music of Buddy Holly	Based on the music of Buddy Holly	Alan Janes Rob Bettinson
Budgie	1988	Mort Shuman	Don Black	Keith Waterhouse Willis Hall
Bugsy Malone	1983	Paul Williams	Paul Williams	Alan Parker
Bye Bye Birdie	1960	Charles Strouse	Lee Adams	Mike Stewart
By Jeeves	1975	Andrew Lloyd Webber	Alan Ayckbourn	Alan Ayckbourn

C

MUSICAL	YEAR	MUSIC	LYRICS	BOOK
Cabaret	1966	John Kander	Fred Ebb	Joe Masteroff
Calamity Jane	1979	Sammy Fain	Paul Francis Webster	Phil Park Ronald Hanmer
Call Me Madam	1950	Irving Berlin	Irving Berlin	Howard Lindsay Russell Crouse
Camelot	1960	Frederick Loewe	Alan Jay Lerner	Alan Jay Lerner
Can Can	1953	Cole Porter	Cole Porter	Abe Burrows
Candide	1956	Leonard Bernstein	Richard Wilbur *(Additional lyrics by Stephen Sondheim and John Latouche)*	Lillian Hellman
Canterbury Tales	1968	John Hawkins Richard Hill	Nevill Coghill	Nevill Coghill Martin Starkie
Card (The)	1973	Tony Hatch Jackie Trent	Tony Hatch Jackie Trent	Keith Waterhouse Willis Hall
Caroline or Change	2004	Jeanine Tesori	Tony Kushner	Tony Kushner Jeanine Tesori
Carousel	1945	Richard Rodgers	Oscar Hammerstein II	Oscar Hammerstein II
Carrie	1988	Michael Gore	Michael Gore Dean Pitchford	Lawrence D Cohen
Cats	1981	Andrew Lloyd Webber	T.S. Eliot *(Additional lyrics by Trevor Nunn & Richard Stilgoe)*	Based on: *Old Possum's Book of Practical Cats.*
Charlie Girl	1965	David Heneker John Taylor	David Heneker John Taylor	Hugh Williams Margaret Williams Ray Cooney
Chess	1986	Benny Andersson Björn Ulvæus	Tim Rice	Tim Rice
Chicago	1975	John Kander	Fred Ebb	Fred Ebb Bob Fosse
Children of Eden	1991	Stephen Schwartz	Stephen Schwartz	John Caird

MUSICAL	YEAR	MUSIC	LYRICS	BOOK
Chitty Chitty Bang Bang	2004	Richard M. Sherman Robert B. Sherman	Richard M. Sherman Robert B. Sherman	Jeremy Sands *(Adapted for the stage)*
Chorus Line (A)	1975	Marvin Hamlisch	Edward Kleban	James Kirkwood Nicholas Dante
City of Angels	1989	Cy Coleman	David Zippel	Larry Gelbart
Closer to Heaven	2001	Neil Tennant Chris Lowe *(Pet Shop Boys)*	Neil Tennant Chris Lowe *(Pet Shop Boys)*	Jonathan Harvey
Coco	1969	André Previn	Alan Jay Lerner	Alan Jay Lerner
Color Purple (The)	2005	Brenda Russell Allee Willis Stephen Bray	Brenda Russell Allee Willis Stephen Bray	Marsha Norman
Company	1970	Stephen Sondheim	Stephen Sondheim	George Furth
Connecticut Yankee	1927	Richard Rodgers	Lorenz Hart	Herbert Fields
Copacabana	1994	Barry Manilow	Bruce Sussman Jack Feldman	Barry Manilow Bruce Sussman Jack Feldman
Crazy for You	1992	George Gershwin	Ira Gershwin	Ken Ludwig
Curtains	2007	John Kander	Fred Ebb *(Additional lyrics by John Kander & Rupert Holmes)*	Rupert Holmes *(Original book & concept by Peter Stone)*

D

MUSICAL	YEAR	MUSIC	LYRICS	BOOK
Daddy Cool	2006	Based on the songs of Boney M & Frank Farian	Based on the songs of Boney M & Frank Farian	Stephen Plaice Amani Naphtali *(Original concept by Mary S. Applegate & Michael Stark)*
Dames at Sea	1968	Jim Wise	George Haimsohn Robin Miller	George Haimsohn Robin Miller
Damn Yankees	1955	Richard Adler Jerry Ross	Richard Adler Jerry Ross	George Abbot Douglas Wallop
Dancing Years (The)	1939	Ivor Novello	Christopher Hassall	Ivor Novello
Desert Song (The)	1926	Sigmund Romberg	Otto Harbach Oscar Hammerstein II Frank Mandel	Otto Harbach Oscar Hammerstein II Frank Mandel
Doctor Dolittle	1998	Leslie Bricusse	Leslie Bricusse	Leslie Bricusse
Dreamgirls	1981	Henry Krieger	Tom Eyen	Tom Eyen

E

MUSICAL	YEAR	MUSIC	LYRICS	BOOK
Evita	1978	Andrew Lloyd Webber	Tim Rice	Tim Rice

48

MUSICAL	YEAR	MUSIC	LYRICS	BOOK
Expresso Bongo	1958	David Heneker Monty Norman	Julian More Monty Norman David Heneker	Wolf Mankowitz Julian More

ℱ

MUSICAL	YEAR	MUSIC	LYRICS	BOOK
Fame	1988	Steven Margoshes (Title song by Dean Pitchford & Michael Gore)	Jacques Levy	José Fernandez
Fantasticks	1960	Harvey Schmidt	Tom Jones	Tom Jones
Fiddler On the Roof	1964	Jerry Bock	Sheldon Harnick	Joseph Stein
Fifty Million Frenchmen	1929	Cole Porter	Cole Porter	Herbert Fields
Fings Ain't Wot They Used T'Be	1959	Lionel Bart	Lionel Bart	Frank Norman
Finian's Rainbow	1947	Burton Lane	E.Y. Harburg	E.Y. Harburg Fred Saidy
Fiorello!	1959	Jerry Bock	Sheldon Harnick	George Abbot Jerome Weidman
Five Guys Named Moe	1990	Featuring Louis Jordan's greatest hits	–	Clark Peters
Fix (The)	1997	Dana P. Rowe	John Dempsey	John Dempsey
Flora the Red Menace	1965	John Kander	Fred Ebb	George Abbott Robert Russell
Flower Drum Song	1958	Richard Rodgers	Oscar Hammerstein II	Oscar Hammerstein II Joseph Fields
Follies	1971	Stephen Sondheim	Stephen Sondheim	James Goldman
Footloose	1998	Eric Carmen Michael Gore Sammy Hagar Kenny Loggins Tom Snow Jim Steinman Bill Wolfer Dean Pitchford	Eric Carmen Michael Gore Sammy Hagar Kenny Loggins Tom Snow Jim Steinman Bill Wolfer Dean Pitchford	Dean Pitchford David Saint
42nd Street	1980	Harry Warren	Al Dubin	Michael Stewart Mark Bramble
Full Monty (The)	2000	David Yazbek	David Yazbek	Terrence McNally
Funny Girl	1964	Jule Styne	Jule Styne	Isobel Lennart
Funny Thing Happened On the Way to the Forum (A)	1962	Stephen Sondheim	Stephen Sondheim	Burt Shevelove Larry Gelbart

MUSICAL	YEAR	MUSIC	LYRICS	BOOK

G

MUSICAL	YEAR	MUSIC	LYRICS	BOOK
Gay Divorce	1932	Cole Porter	Cole Porter	Kenneth Webb Samuel Hoffenstein
Gentlemen Prefer Blondes	1949	Jule Styne	Leo Robin	Joseph Fields Anita Loos
Gigi	1973	Frederick Loewe	Alan Jay Lerner	Alan Jay Lerner
Girlfriend (The)	1926	Richard Rodgers	Lorenz Hart	Herbert Fields
Godspell	1971	Stephen Schwartz	Stephen Schwartz (New Lyric)	Conceived by John-Michael Tebelak
Gone with the Wind	2008	Margaret Martin	Margaret Martin	Aldo Scrofani Trevor Nunn
Goodbye Girl (The)	1993	Marvin Hamlisch	David Zippel	Neil Simon
Grand Hotel	1989	George Forrest Robert Wright (Additional Music by Maury Yeston)	George Forrest Robert Wright (Additional Lyrics by Maury Yeston)	Luther Davis
Grease	1972	Jim Jacobs Warren Casey	Jim Jacobs Warren Casey	Jim Jacobs Warren Casey
Guys and Dolls	1950	Frank Loesser	Frank Loesser	Jo Swerling Abe Burrows
Gypsy	1959	Jule Styne	Stephen Sondheim	Arthur Laurents

H

MUSICAL	YEAR	MUSIC	LYRICS	BOOK
Hair	1967	Galt MacDermot	Gerome Ragni James Rado	Gerome Ragni James Rado
Hairspray	2002	Marc Shaiman	Scott Wittman Marc Shaiman	Mark O'Donnell Thomas Meehan
Half a Sixpence	1963	David Heneker	David Heneker	Beverly Cross
Hallelujah Baby	1967	Jule Styne	Betty Comden Adolph Green	Arthur Laurents
Hello Dolly	1964	Jerry Herman	Jerry Herman	Michael Stewart
High Society	1987	Cole Porter	Cole Porter	Richard Eyre
Hired Man (The)	1984	Howard Goodall	Melvyn Bragg	Melvyn Bragg
Honk!	1993	George Stiles	Anthony Drewe	Anthony Drewe
Hot Mikado	1939	Music adapted & arranged by Rob Bowman (Revised version: based on The Mikado by W.S. Gilbert and Arthur Sullivan)	David H. Bell (Revised version: based on The Mikado by W.S. Gilbert and Arthur Sullivan)	David H. Bell (Revised version: based on The Mikado by W.S. Gilbert and Arthur Sullivan)

MUSICAL	YEAR	MUSIC	LYRICS	BOOK
How to Succeed in Business Without Really Trying	1961	Frank Loesser	Frank Loesser	Abe Burrows Jack Weinstocks Willie Gilbert

I

MUSICAL	YEAR	MUSIC	LYRICS	BOOK
I Love You, You're Perfect, Now Change	1996	Jimmy Roberts	Joe Dipietro	Joe Dipietro
Into the Woods	1986	Stephen Sondheim	Stephen Sondheim	James Lapine

J

MUSICAL	YEAR	MUSIC	LYRICS	BOOK
Jailhouse Rock	2004	Based on songs made famous by Elvis Presley and others and written by various writers	Based on songs made famous by Elvis Presley and others and written by various writers	Rob Bettinson Alan Janes
Jekyll and Hyde	1997	Frank Wildhorn	Leslie Bricusse	Leslie Bricusse
Jerry Springer the Opera	2003	Richard Thomas	Stewart Lee Richard Thomas	Stewart Lee Richard Thomas
Jersey Boys	2005	Bob Gaudio	Bob Crewe	Marshall Brickman Rick Elice
Jesus Christ Superstar	1971	Andrew Lloyd Webber	Tim Rice	Tim Rice
Joseph and the Amazing Technicolor Dreamcoat	1968	Andrew Lloyd Webber	Tim Rice	Tim Rice
Jubilee	1935	Cole Porter	Cole Porter	Moss Hart
Just So	1984	George Stiles	Anthony Drewe	Anthony Drewe

K

MUSICAL	YEAR	MUSIC	LYRICS	BOOK
King & I (The)	1951	Richard Rodgers	Oscar Hammerstein II	Oscar Hammerstein II
King's Rhapsody	1949	Ivor Novello	Christopher Hassall	Ivor Novello
Kismet	1953	Robert Wright George Forrest (From the themes of Alexander Borodin)	Robert Wright George Forrest (From the themes of Alexander Borodin)	Charles Lederer Luther Davis
Kiss Me Kate	1948	Cole Porter	Cole Porter	Bella and Samuel Spewack
Kiss of the Spiderwoman	1992	John Kander	Fred Ebb	Terrence McNally

L

MUSICAL	YEAR	MUSIC	LYRICS	BOOK
La Cage aux Folles	1983	Jerry Herman	Jerry Herman	Harvey Fierstein

MUSICAL	YEAR	MUSIC	LYRICS	BOOK
La Cava	2000	Laurence O'Keefe Stephen Keeling *(Additional music by John Cameron)*	John Claflin Laurence O'Keefe *(Additional lyrics by Shaun McKenna)*	Dana Broccoli
Lady be Good	1924	George Gershwin	Ira Gershwin	Guy Bolton Fred Thompson
Lady in the Dark	1941	Kurt Weill	Ira Gershwin	Moss Hart
Last Five Years (The)	2001	Jason Robert Brown	Jason Robert Brown	Jason Robert Brown
Leave It to Me	1938	Cole Porter	Cole Porter	Bella Spewack Samuel Spewack
Legally Blonde	2007	Laurence O'Keefe Nell Benjamin	Laurence O'Keefe Nell Benjamin	Heather Hach
Les Misérables	1985	Claude-Michel Schönberg	Herbert Kretzmer Alain Boublil	Alain Boublil Claude-Michel Schönberg
Let 'Em Eat Cake	1933	George Gershwin	Ira Gershwin	George S. Kaufman Morrie Ryskind
Let's Face It	1941	Cole Porter	Cole Porter	Herbert & Dorothy Fields
Life (The)	1997	Cy Coleman	Ira Gasman	David Newman Ira Gasman Cy Coleman
Lion King (The)	1997	Elton John	Tim Rice *(Additional music and lyrics by: Lebo M Mark Mancina Jay Rifkin Julie Taymore Hans Zimmer)*	Roger Allers Irene Mecchi
Little Me	1962	Cy Coleman	Carolyn Leigh	Neil Simon
Little Mermaid (The)	2007	Alan Menken	Howard Ashman Glen Slater	Doug Wright
Little Night Music (A)	1973	Stephen Sondheim	Stephen Sondheim	Hugh Wheeler
Little Shop of Horrors (The)	1982	Alan Menken	Howard Ashman	Howard Ashman
Lord of the Rings	2006	A.R. Rahman Värttinä	Matthew Warchus Shaun McKenna	Matthew Warchus Shaun McKenna

M

Mack and Mabel	1974	Jerry Herman	Jerry Herman	Michael Stewart
Maggie May	1964	Lionel Bart	Lionel Bart	Alun Owen
Mame	1966	Jerry Herman	Jerry Herman	Jerome Lawrence Robert E. Lee

MUSICAL	YEAR	MUSIC	LYRICS	BOOK
Mamma Mia	1999	ABBA Björn Ulvaeus Benny Andersson	ABBA Björn Ulvaeus Benny Andersson	Catherine Johnson
Man of La Mancha	1965	Mitch Leigh	Joe Darion	Dale Wasserman
Marguerite	2008	Michael Legrand	Herbert Kretzmer	Alain Boublil Claude-Michel Schönberg Jonathan Kent
Martin Guerre	1996	Claude-Michel Schönberg	Edward Hardy Stephen Clark *(Additional lyrics by* *Herbert Kretzmer &* *Alain Boublil)*	Alain Boublil Claude-Michel Schönberg
Mary Poppins	2004	Richard M. Sherman Robert R. Sherman	Richard M. Sherman Robert R. Sherman	Julian Fellowes
Matchgirls (The)	1966	Tony Russell	Bill Owen	Bill Owen
Me and My Girl	1937	Noel Gay	L. Arthur Rose Douglas Furber	L. Arthur Rose Douglas Furber
Meet Me in St Louis	1989	Hugh Martin Ralph Blane	Hugh Martin Ralph Blane	Sally Benson
Merrily We Roll *Along*	1981	Stephen Sondheim	Stephen Sondheim	George Furth
Metropolis	1989	Joe Brooks	Dusty Hughes Joe Brooks	Dusty Hughes Joe Brooks
Miss Saigon	1989	Claude-Michel Schönberg	Alain Boublil Richard Maltby Jr	Alain Boublil, Claude-Michel Schönberg *(Additional* *material: Richard* *Maltby Jr)*
Moby Dick	1992	Hereward Kaye Robert Longden	Robert Longden *(Additional lyrics by* *Hereward Kaye)*	Robert Longden
Movin' Out	2002	Based on the music and lyrics of Billy Joel	Based on the music and lyrics of Billy Joel	Conceived by Twyla Tharp
Mr Cinders	1929	Vivian Ellis Richard Myers	Clifford Grey Greatrex Newman *(Additional lyrics by* *Leo Robin & Vivian Ellis)*	Clifford Grey Greatrex Newman
Music in the Air	1932	Jerome Kern	Oscar Hammerstein II	Oscar Hammerstein II
Music Man (The)	1957	Meredith Willson	Meredith Willson	Meredith Willson
My Fair Lady	1956	Frederick Loewe	Alan Jay Lerner	Alan Jay Lerner
My Favourite Year	1992	Stephen Flaherty	Lynn Ahrens	Joseph Dougherty
My One and Only	1983	George Gershwin	Ira Gershwin	Peter Stone Timothy S. Mayer

MUSICAL	YEAR	MUSIC	LYRICS	BOOK
Mystery of Edwin Drood (The)	1985	Rupert Holmes	Rupert Holmes	Rupert Holmes

N

MUSICAL	YEAR	MUSIC	LYRICS	BOOK
Never Forget	2008	Based on the music of Take That	Based on the music of Take That	Danny Brocklehurst
Nine	1982	Arthur Kopit	Maury Yeston	Maury Yeston
No, No, Nanette	1925	Vincent Youmans	Irving Caesar Otto Harbach	Otto Harbach Frank Mandel
No Strings	1962	Richard Rodgers	Richard Rodgers	Samuel Taylor
Notre Dame de Paris	1998	Richard Cocciante (English lyrics by Will Jennings)	Luc Plamondon	Luc Plamondon

O

MUSICAL	YEAR	MUSIC	LYRICS	BOOK
Of Thee I Sing	1931	George Gershwin	Ira Gershwin	George S. Kaufman Morrie Ryskind
Oh, Kay!	1926	George Gershwin	Ira Gershwin	Guy Bolton P.G. Wodehouse
Oklahoma!	1943	Richard Rodgers	Oscar Hammerstein II	Oscar Hammerstein II
Oliver!	1960	Lionel Bart	Lionel Bart	Lionel Bart
Once On This Island	1990	Stephen Flaherty	Lynn Ahrens	Lynn Ahrens
On the Town	1944	Leonard Bernstein	Betty Comden Adolph Green	Betty Comden Adolph Green
On Your Toes	1936	Richard Rodgers	Lorenz Hart	Richard Rodgers Lorenz Hart George Abbott

P

MUSICAL	YEAR	MUSIC	LYRICS	BOOK
Pacific Overtures	1976	Stephen Sondheim	Stephen Sondheim	John Weidman (Additional material by Hugh Wheeler)
Paint Your Wagon	1951	Frederick Loewe	Alan Jay Lerner	Alan Jay Lerner
Pajama Game (The)	1954	Richard Adler Jerry Ross	Richard Adler Jerry Ross	George Abbott Richard Bissell
Pal Joey	1940	Richard Rodgers	Lorenz Hart	John O'Hara
Parade	1998	Jason Robert Brown	Jason Robert Brown	Alfred Uhry
Passion	1994	Stephen Sondheim	Stephen Sondheim	James Lapine
Perchance to Dream	1945	Ivor Novello	Ivor Novello	Ivor Novello

MUSICAL	YEAR	MUSIC	LYRICS	BOOK
Phantom of the Opera (The)	1986	Andrew Lloyd Webber	Charles Hart (Additional lyrics by Richard Stilgoe)	Andrew Lloyd Webber Richard Stilgoe
Pickwick	1963	Cyril Ornadel	Leslie Bricusse	Wolf Mankowitz
Pipe Dream	1955	Richard Rodgers	Oscar Hammerstein II	Oscar Hammerstein II
Pippin	1972	Stephen Schwartz	Stephen Schwartz	Roger O. Hirson
Pirate Queen (The)	2006	Claude-Michel Schönberg	Alain Boublil Richard Maltby Jr John Dempsey	Claude-Michel Schönberg Alain Boublil Richard Maltby Jr
Porgy and Bess	1935	George Gershwin	Ira Gershwin	DuBose Heyward
Producers (The)	2001	Mel Brooks	Mel Brooks	Mel Brooks Thomas Meehan

R

MUSICAL	YEAR	MUSIC	LYRICS	BOOK
Rags	1986	Charles Strouse	Stephen Schwartz	Joseph Stein
Ragtime	1998	Stephen Flaherty	Lynn Ahrens	Terrence McNally
Rent	1995	Jonathan Larson	Jonathan Larson	Jonathan Larson
Return to the Forbidden Planet	1989	Various Artists	Various Artists	Bob Carlton
Rink (The)	1984	John Kander	Fred Ebb	Terence McNally
Roar of the Greasepaint – The Smell of the Crowd (The)	1964	Leslie Bricusse Anthony Newley	Leslie Bricusse Anthony Newley	Leslie Bricusse Anthony Newley
Robert and Elizabeth	1964	Ron Grainer	Ronald Millar	Ronald Millar
Rocky Horror Picture Show (The)	1973	Richard O'Brien	Richard O'Brien	Richard O'Brien

S

MUSICAL	YEAR	MUSIC	LYRICS	BOOK
Salad Days	1954	Julian Slade	Dorothy Reynolds Julian Slade	Dorothy Reynolds Julian Slade
Sally	1920	Jerome Kern (Ballet music by Victor Herbert)	Clifford Grey Anne Caldwell P.G. Wodehouse Buddy G. DeSylva	Guy Bolton
Saturday Night Fever	1998	Bee Gees	Bee Gees	Stage adaptation by Nan Knighton
Scarlet Pimpernel (The)	1997	Frank Wildhorn	Nan Knighton	Nan Knighton
Scrooge	1992	Leslie Bricusse	Leslie Bricusse	Leslie Bricusse
Secret Garden (The)	1991	Lucy Simon	Marsha Norman	Marsha Norman
Seesaw	1973	Cy Coleman	Dorothy Fields	Michael Stewart
Seven Brides for Seven Brothers	1982	Gene de Paul	Johnny Mercer	Lawrence Kasha David Landay

MUSICAL	YEAR	MUSIC	LYRICS	BOOK
1776	1969	Sherman Edwards	Sherman Edwards	Peter Stone (Based on. a concept by Sherman Edwards)
70 Girls 70	1971	John Kander	Fred Ebb	Fred Ebb Norman L. Martin (Adapted from Peter Coke's Breath of Spring by Joe Masteroff)
She Loves Me	1963	Jerry Bock	Sheldon Harnick	Joe Masteroff
Show Boat	1927	Jerome Kern & others	Oscar Hammerstein II	Oscar Hammerstein II
Silk Stockings	1955	Cole Porter	Cole Porter	George S. Kaufman Leueen MacGrath Abe Burrows
Singin' in the Rain	1983	Nacio Herb Brown	Arthur Freed	Betty Comden Adolph Green
Snoopy	1982	Larry Grossman	Hal Hackaday	Charles M. Schulz Creative Associates: Warren Lockhart Arthur Whitelaw Michael L. Grace
Some Like It Hot	1972	Jule Styne	Bob Merrill	Peter Stone
Song of Norway	1944	Edvard Grieg	Robert Wright George Forrest (Lyrics & musical adaptation)	Milton Lazarus
Songs for a New World	1995	Jason Robert Brown	Jason Robert Brown	Conceived by Daisy Prince
Sound of Music (The)	1959	Richard Rodgers	Oscar Hammerstein II	Howard Lindsay Russell Crouse
South Pacific	1948	Richard Rodgers	Oscar Hammerstein II	Oscar Hammerstein II Joshua Logan
Spamalot	2005	John Du Prez Eric Idle	Eric Idle	Eric Idle
Spend Spend Spend	1998	Steve Brown	Steve Brown	Steve Brown Justin Greene
Spring Awakening	2006	Duncan Sheik	Steven Sater	Steven Sater
Starlight Express	1984	Andrew Lloyd Webber	Richard Stilgoe	Based on an idea by Andrew Lloyd Webber
State Fair	1996	Richard Rodgers	Oscar Hammerstein II	Tom Briggs Louis Mattioli

MUSICAL	YEAR	MUSIC	LYRICS	BOOK
Stepping Out	1996	Denis King	Mary Stewart-David	Richard Harris
Stop the World – I Want to Get Off	1961	Leslie Bricusse Anthony Newley	Leslie Bricusse Anthony Newley	Leslie Bricusse Anthony Newley
Strike Up the Band	1930	George Gershwin	Ira Gershwin	Morrie Ryskind
Sunday in the Park with George	1984	Stephen Sondheim	Stephen Sondheim	James Lapine
Sunny	1925	Jerome Kern	Oscar Hammerstein II Otto Harbach	Oscar Hammerstein II Otto Harbach
Sunset Boulevard	1993	Andrew Lloyd Webber	Christopher Hampton Don Black	Christopher Hampton Don Black
Sweeney Todd	1979	Stephen Sondheim	Stephen Sondheim	Hugh Wheeler
Sweet Charity	1966	Cy Coleman	Dorothy Fields	Neil Simon

T

MUSICAL	YEAR	MUSIC	LYRICS	BOOK
Taboo	2002	Boy George Kevan Frost	Boy George	Mark Davies
Tell Me On a Sunday	1980	Andrew Lloyd Webber	Don Black	–
They're Playing Our Song	1979	Marvin Hamlisch	Carol Bayer Sager	Neil Simon
13	2007	Jason Robert Brown	Jason Robert Brown	Dan Elish
Thoroughly Modern Millie	2002	Jeanine Tesori (new music)	Dick Scanlan (new lyrics)	Richard D. Morris Dick Scanlan
Tick Tick Boom	2001	Jonathan Larson	Jonathan Larson	Jonathan Larson
Time	1986	Jeff Daniels	David Soames	Devised and created by Dave Clark
Titanic	1999	Maury Yeston	Maury Yeston	Peter Stone
Tommy	1979	Pete Townshend The Who (Additional music: John Entwhistle & Keith Moon)	Pete Townshend The Who (Additional music: John Entwhistle & Keith Moon)	Pete Townshend Des McAnuff
25th Annual Putnam County Spelling Bee	2005	William Finn	William Finn	Rachel Sheinkin
Two Gentlemen of Verona	1971	Galt MacDermot	John Guare	John Guare Mel Shapiro

U

MUSICAL	YEAR	MUSIC	LYRICS	BOOK
Vagabond King (The)	1925	Rudolf Friml	W.H. Post Brian Hooker	W.H. Post Brian Hooker
Victor Victoria	1995	Henry Mancini	Leslie Bricusse	Blake Edwards

MUSICAL	YEAR	MUSIC	LYRICS	BOOK
𝒲				
We Will Rock You	2002	Queen	Queen	Ben Elton
West Side Story	1957	Leonard Bernstein	Stephen Sondheim	Arthur Laurents
Wicked	2003	Stephen Schwartz	Stephen Schwartz	–
Wild Party (The)	2000	Andrew Lippa	Andrew Lippa	Andrew Lippa
Will Rogers Follies	1991	Cy Coleman	Betty Comden Adolph Green	Peter Stone (Inspired by the words of Will & Betty Rogers)
Witches of Eastwick	2000	Dana Rowe	John Dempsey	John Dempsey
Wiz (The)	1975	Charlie Smalls	Charlie Smalls	William F. Brown
Wizard of Oz (The) (stage Version)	1903	A. Baldwin Sloane Paul Tietjens	Frank Baum	Frank Baum
Woman in White (The)	2004	Andrew Lloyd Webber	David Zippel	Charlotte Jones
Woman of the Year	1981	John Kander	Fred Ebb	Peter Stone
Wonderful Town	1978	Leonard Bernstein	Betty Comden Adolph Green	Joseph Fields Jerome Chodorov
Working	1978	Craig Camelia Micki Grant Mary Rodgers Susan Birkenhead Stephen Schwartz James Taylor	Craig Camelia Micki Grant Mary Rodgers Susan Birkenhead Stephen Schwartz James Taylor	Adapted by Stephen Schwartz
𝒳				
Xanadu	2007	John Farrar Jeff Lynne	John Farrar Jeff Lynne	Douglas Carter Beane
𝒴				
Young Frankenstein	2007	Mel Brooks	Mel Brooks	Mel Brooks Thomas Meehan
𝒵				
Zorba	1968	John Kander	Fred Ebb	Joseph Stein

Chronological List of Popular Musicals

I am frequently asked the question: 'What musicals were written in the 40s, 50s, 60s etc?'. This section will enable you to check in what year a musical was given its first stage production, whilst at the same time noting how popular the stage musical has become. One wonders how many more will be added to the list before the 'noughties' comes to an end. Only the most popular musicals are listed here.

1920s

Bitter Sweet • Connecticut Yankees • Desert Song (The) • Fifty Million Frenchmen • Lady be Good • Mr Cinders • No, No, Nanette • Oh, Kay! • Sally • Show Boat • Sunny • Threepenny Opera • Vagabond King (The)

1930s

Anything Goes • Babes in Arms • Boys From Syracuse (The) • Dancing Years (The) • Gay Divorce • Hot Mikado • Jubilee • Leave It to Me • Let 'Em Eat Cake • Me and My Girl • Music in the Air • Of Thee I Sing • On Your Toes • Porgy and Bess • Strike Up the Band

1940s

Allegro • Annie Get Your Gun • Bless the Bride • Brigadoon • Carousel • Finian's Rainbow • Gentlemen Prefer Blondes • King's Rhapsody • Kiss Me Kate • Lady in the Dark • Let's Face It • Oklahoma! • On the Town • On Your Toes • Pal Joey • Perchance to Dream • Song of Norway • South Pacific

1950s

Bells are Ringing (The) • Boyfriend (The) • Call Me Madam • Can Can • Candide • Caroline or Change • Damn Yankees • Expresso Bongo • Fings Ain't Wot They Used T'Be • Fiorello! • Flower Drum Song • Guys and Dolls • Gypsy • King and I (The) • Kismet • Music Man (The) • My Fair Lady • Paint Your Wagon • Pajama Game (The) • Pipe Dream • Salad Days • Silk Stockings • Sound of Music (The) • West Side Story

1960s

Anyone Can Whistle • Blitz • Bye Bye Birdie • Cabaret • Camelot • Canterbury Tales • Charlie Girl • Coco • Dames at Sea • Fantasticks • Fiddler On the Roof • Funny Girl • Funny Thing Happened On the Way to the Forum (A) • Hair • Half a Sixpence • Hallelujah Baby • Hello Dolly • How to Succeed in Business Without Really Trying • Joseph and the Amazing Technicolor Dreamcoat • Little Me • Mame • Man of La Mancha • Matchgirls (The) • No Strings • Oliver! • Pickwick • Roar of the

Greasepaint – The Smell of the Crowd (The) • *Robert and Elizabeth* • *She Loves Me* • *Stop the World – I Want to Get Off* • *Sweet Charity* • *Zorba*

1970s

Act (The) • *Annie* • *Applause* • *Best Little Whorehouse in Texas (The)* • *Billy* • *By Jeeves* • *Calamity Jane* • *Card (The)* • *Chicago* • *Chorus Line (A)* • *Company* • *Evita* • *Follies* • *Gigi* • *Godspell* • *Grease* • *Jesus Christ Superstar* • *Little Night Music (A)* • *Mack and Mabel* • *Rocky Horror Picture Show (The)* • *Seesaw* • *70 Girls 70* • *Sweeney Todd* • *They're Playing Our Song* • *Tommy* • *Wiz (The)*

1980s

Aspects of Love • *Baby* • *Baker's Wife (The)* • *Barnum* • *Big River* • *Blondel* • *Blood Brothers* • *Buddy* • *Budgie* • *Bugsy Malone* • *Carrie* • *Cats* • *Chess* • *City of Angels* • *Dreamgirls* • *Fame* • *42nd Street* • *Grand Hotel* • *High Society* • *Hired Man* • *Into the Woods* • *Just So* • *La Cage aux Folles* • *Les Misérables* • *Little Shop of Horrors (The)* • *Meet Me in St Louis* • *Merrily We Roll Along* • *Metropolis* • *Miss Saigon* • *My One and Only* • *Mystery of Edwin Drood (The)* • *Nine* • *Phantom of the Opera (The)* • *Rags* • *Return to the Forbidden Planet* • *Rink (The)* • *Seven Brides for Seven Brothers* • *Singin' in the Rain* • *Starlight Express* • *Sunday in the Park with George* • *Tell Me On a Sunday*

1990s

Assassins • *Beauty and the Beast* • *Bernadette* • *Children of Eden* • *Copacabana* • *Crazy for You* • *Doctor Dolittle* • *Five Guys Named Moe* • *Fix (The)* • *Footloose* • *Honk* • *Jekyll and Hyde* • *Kiss of the Spiderwoman* • *Life (The)* • *Lion King (The)* • *Mamma Mia* • *Martin Guerre* • *Moby Dick* • *My Favourite Year* • *Notre Dame de Paris* • *Once On This Island* • *Parade* • *Passion* • *Ragtime* • *Rent* • *Saturday Night Fever* • *Scarlet Pimpernel* • *Scrooge* • *Secret Garden (The)* • *Spend Spend Spend* • *Stepping Out* • *Sunset Boulevard*

2000s

Acorn Antiques • *Avenue Q* • *Bad Girls – The Musical* • *Bat Boy* • *Beautiful Game (The)* • *Big the Musical* • *Billy Elliot* • *Bombay Dreams* • *Bounce* • *Chitty Chitty Bang Bang* • *Closer to Heaven* • *Color Purple (The)* • *Curtains* • *Daddy Cool* • *Drowsy Chaperone* • *Full Monty (The)* • *Gone with the Wind* • *Hairspray* • *High School Musical* • *Jailhouse Rock*

• *Jerry Springer the Opera* • *Jersey Boys* • *La Cava* • *Last Five Years (The)* • *Legally Blonde* • *Little Mermaid (The)* • *Lord of the Rings (The)* • *Marguerite* • *Mary Poppins* • *Movin' Out* • *Never Forget* • *Parade* • *Pirate Queen (The)* • *Producers (The)* • *Spamalot* • *Spring Awakening* • *Taboo* • *Thoroughly Modern Millie* • *Tick Tick Boom* • *Titanic* • *We Will Rock You* • *Wicked* • *Wild Party* • *Witches of Eastwick* • *Woman in White (The)* • *Xanadu* • *Young Frankenstein*

Categorised Section

Maybe you want to know what type of musical it is that you are going to see or that your local group wants to produce? To answer these questions, here are just some of the musicals categorised. Categorising in this way can be surprisingly useful, even if to just organise your soundtracks into some sort of logical order, other than alphabetical. This is a section you can keep and then add to in the future, but do note that some musicals can fit comfortably into more than one category.

Classic

These are suitable for the real musical lovers and many are available for amateur productions.

Annie Get Your Gun; Anything Goes; Bless the Bride; Boyfriend (The); Brigadoon; Cabaret; Calamity Jane; Carousel; Dancing Years (The); Desert Song (The); Gigi; Guys and Dolls; Gypsy; Half a Sixpence; Hello Dolly; High Society; King and I (The); Kiss Me Kate; Me and My Girl; My Fair Lady; Seven Brides for Seven Brothers; Singin' in the Rain; Sound of Music (The); South Pacific; West Side Story; Wizard of Oz (The)

Child Friendly

These musicals all either have child parts (and, as we know, children love watching other children on the stage) or they are particulary suitable for children.

Annie; Billy Elliot; Bugsy Malone; Chitty Chitty Bang Bang; Doctor Dolittle; Joseph and the Amazing Technicolor Dreamcoat; King and I (The); Lion King (The); Little Mermaid (The); Mary Poppins; Oliver!; Scrooge; Secret Garden (The); Sound of Music (The); South Pacific; Wicked; Wizard of Oz (The)

Dancers

Musicals which require an above average standard of dance are in this category.

Billy Elliot; Cats; Chicago; Chorus Line (A); Contact; Footloose; 42nd Street; Movin' Out; On the Town; Saturday Night Fever; West Side Story

Cult

This type of musical attracts an audience who return again and again, generally because it either involves audience participation or a lot of singing along!

Buddy; Hair; Mamma Mia; Never Forget; Rocky Horror Picture Show (The)

Rock

Often very noisy and always atmospheric, these musicals sometimes have a cult following too because of their huge fan base.

Godspell; Hair; Jesus Christ Superstar; Tommy; Tonight's the Night; We Will Rock You

Skills

Musicals to be admired because they require a multi-skilled and talented cast.

Barnum (Circus)*; Buddy* (Musicians)*; Return to the Forbidden Planet* (Musicians)*; Starlight Express* (Roller skates)

Westerns

The old cowboy type musical.

Annie Get Your Gun; Calamity Jane; Oklahoma!; Paint Your Wagon; Seven Brides for Seven Brothers

Comedies

Funny, but only if it is your sense of humour!

Acorn Antiques; Avenue Q; Full Monty (The); Funny Thing Happened On the Way to the Forum (A); Hairspray; Jerry Springer the Opera; La Cage aux Folles; Little Shop of Horrors (The); Producers (The); Return to the Forbidden Planet; Rocky Horror Picture Show (The); Spamalot

Heavies

Musicals which require some thought, or at least attention! You can't let your mind wander during these.

Aspects of Love; Evita; Fiddler On the Roof; Into the Woods; Last Five Years (The); Les Misérables; Little Night Music (A); Lord of the Rings (The); Merrily We Roll Along; Miss Saigon; Parade; Phantom of the Opera (The); Porgy and Bess; Rent; Show Boat; Sunset Boulevard; Sweeney Todd; Tommy; West Side Story; Woman in White (The)

Weepies

When you go to see one of these, you'll need to bring a very large box of tissues with you!

Blood Brothers; Evita; Gypsy; King and I (The)

True Stories

You need to know if you are going to see a musical based on a true story because it certainly makes you view it differently.

Annie Get Your Gun; Evita; Gypsy; King and I (The); Parade

Sourcing a Musical

WHAT COMES FIRST?

What comes first, the music or the lyrics? In terms of writing a song, every composer and lyricist on the planet must have been asked this question. The answer is simple; whatever takes your fancy, because there is no set rule. However, where the writing of a musical is concerned, that's completely different and it has nothing to do with 'whatever takes your fancy', rather it is a game full of rules; break them and you lose, for most creators of musical theatre seem to agree that, when writing a musical, what comes first is the book.

Tim Rice once famously said in answer to the question: 'What makes a good musical?' 'The book, the book . . . and the book!' It is a belief shared by most creators of musical theatre. The question now becomes what makes a good storyline and where do the creators come up with their ideas? As well as being the most important ingredient, the idea is also the most difficult and unique; ground-breaking ideas are very rare. Once someone comes up with an idea, then we are inundated with numerous copy cat ideas. Apparently, after the success of the musical *Cats*, producer Cameron Mackintosh was inundated with new ideas for musicals based on dogs!

It would seem that there are a handful of standard ways of sourcing subject matter for new musicals and that there are very few new works written from scratch. So take a look at the following table of standard source *factories* and the musicals which emerged as a result.

MUSICALS BASED ON LITERATURE

There is of course an unlimited supply of exciting 'stories' from this source, because there is a vast amount of readily available literature. Note, 'Nov' is short for novel.

MUSICAL	BASED ON NOVELS OR STAGE PLAYS
Aspects of Love	**(Nov)** Aspects of Love by David Garnett
Big River	**(Nov)** The Adventures of Huckleberry Finn by Mark Twain
Billy	**(Nov)** Billy Liar by Keith Waterhouse & Willis Hall
Boys From Syracuse (The)	**(Play)** Comedy of Errors by William Shakespeare
By Jeeves	**(Nov)** The Jeeves Stories by P.G. Wodehouse
Cabaret	**(Play)** I Am a Camera by John van Druten &
	(Nov) The Berlin Stories by Christopher Isherwood
Camelot	**(Nov)** The Once And Future King by T.H. White
Candide	**(Nov)** Candide by Voltaire
Card (The)	**(Nov)** The Card by Arnold Bennett
Carousel	**(Play)** Liliom by Ferenc Molnar
Carrie	**(Nov)** Carrie by Stephen King
Cats	**(Poem)** Old Possum's Book of Practical Cats by T.S. Eliot
Chicago	**(Play)** Chicago by Maurine Dallas Watkins
Color Purple (The)	**(Nov)** The Color Purple by Alice Walker
Damn Yankees	**(Nov)** The Year the Yankees Lost the Pennant by Douglas Wallop
Doctor Dolittle	**(Nov)** The Doctor Dolittle Stories by Hugh Lofting
Dracula	**(Nov)** Dracula by Bram Stoker
Fiddler On the Roof	**(Nov)** Based on stories by Sholem Aleichem
Flora the Red Menace	**(Nov)** Love is Just Around the Corner by Lester Atwell
Flower Drum Song	**(Nov)** Flower Drum Song by C.Y. Lee
42nd Street	**(Nov)** 42nd Street by Bradford Ropes

MUSICAL	BASED ON NOVELS OR STAGE PLAYS
Funny Thing Happened On the Way to the Forum (A)	**(Play)** Based on the plays of Plautus
Gentlemen Prefer Blondes	**(Nov)** Gentlemen Prefer Blondes by Anita Loos
Gigi	**(Nov)** Gigi by Colette
Gone with the Wind	**(Nov)** Gone with the Wind by Margaret Mitchell
Grand Hotel	**(Nov)** Grand Hotel by Vicki Baum
Guys and Dolls	**(Nov)** Based on stories by Damon Runyon
Half a Sixpence	**(Nov)** Kipps by H.G. Wells
Hello Dolly	**(Play)** The Matchmaker by Thornton Wilder
High Society	**(Play)** The Philadelphia Story by Philip Barry
Hired Man (The)	**(Nov)** The Hired Man by Melvyn Bragg
How to Succeed in Business Without Really Trying	**(Nov)** How to Succeed in Business Without Really Trying by Shepherd Mead
Jekyll and Hyde	**(Nov)** The Strange Case of Doctor Jekyll and Mr Hyde by Robert Louis Stevenson
Just So	**(Nov)** Just So Stories by Rudyard Kipling
King and I (The)	**(Nov)** Anna and the King of Siam by Margaret Landon
Kismet	**(Play)** Kismet by Edward Knoblock
Kiss Me Kate	**(Play)** The Taming of the Shrew by William Shakespeare
Kiss of the Spider Woman	**(Nov)** Kiss of the Spider Woman by Manuel Puig
La Cage aux Folles	**(Play)** La Cage aux Folles by Jean Poiret
La Cava	**(Nov)** La Cava by Dana Broccoli
Leave It to Me	**(Play)** Clear All Wires by Bella & Sam Spewack
Legally Blonde	**(Nov)** Legally Blonde by Amanda Brown
Les Misérables	**(Nov)** Les Misérables by Victor Hugo
Lestat	**(Nov)** The Vampire Chronicles by Anne Rice
Let's Face It	**(Play)** The Cradle Snatchers by Russell Medcraft & Norma Mitchell
Little Me	**(Nov)** Little Me by Patrick Dennis
Mame	**(Play)** Auntie Mame by Jerome Lawrence & Robert E. Lee
Marguerite	**(Nov)** La Dame aux Camelias by Alexandre Dumas
Mary Poppins	**(Nov)** Based on the stories of P.L. Travers
Meet Me in St Louis	**(Nov)** Kensington Stories by Sally Benson
Merrily We Roll Along	**(Play)** Merrily We Roll Along by George S. Kaufman & Moss Hart
Moby Dick	**(Nov)** Moby Dick by Herman Melville
My Fair Lady	**(Play)** Pygmalion by George Bernard Shaw
Notre Dame de Paris	**(Nov)** Notre Dame de Paris by Victor Hugo
Oklahoma!	**(Nov)** Green Grow the Lilacs by Lynn Riggs
Oliver!	**(Nov)** Oliver Twist by Charles Dickens
Once On this Island	**(Nov)** My Love, My Love by Rosa Guy

MUSICAL	BASED ON NOVELS OR STAGE PLAYS
Pajama Game (The)	**(Nov)** Seven and a Half Cents by Richard Bissell
Pal Joey	**(Nov)** Based on the short stories by John O'Hara
Phantom of the Opera (The)	**(Nov)** Phantom of the Opera by Gaston Leroux
Pickwick	**(Nov)** Based on The Posthumous Papers of the Pickwick Club by Charles Dickens
Pipe Dream	**(Nov)** Sweet Thursday by John Steinbeck
Pirate Queen (The)	**(Nov)** Grania: She-King of the Irish Seas by Morgan Llywelyn
Porgy and Bess	**(Play)** Porgy by Dubose & Dorothy Heyward
Ragtime	**(Nov)** Ragtime by E.L. Doctorow
Robert and Elizabeth	**(Nov)** The Barretts of Wimpole Street by Rudolph Besier
Scarlet Pimpernel (The)	**(Nov)** The Scarlet Pimpernel by Baroness Orczy
Scrooge	**(Nov)** A Christmas Carol by Charles Dickens
Secret Garden (The)	**(Nov)** The Secret Garden by Frances Hodgson Burnett
Seesaw	**(Play)** Two For the Seasaw by William Gibson
70 Girls 70	**(Play)** Breath of Spring by Peter Coke
She Loves Me	**(Play)** The Honest Finder by Miklos Laszlo
Show Boat	**(Nov)** Show Boat by Edna Ferber
Song of Norway	**(Play)** Song of Norway by Homer Curran
South Pacific	**(Nov)** Tales of the South Pacific by James Michener
Spend Spend Spend	**(Nov)** Spend Spend Spend by Viv Nicholson & Stephen Smith
Spring Awakening	**(Play)** Spring Awakening by Frank Wedekind
State Fair	**(Nov)** State Fair by Phil Stong
Stepping Out	**(Play)** Stepping Out by Richard Harris
Strike Up the Band	**(Nov)** Strike Up the Band by George S. Kaufman
Two Gentlemen of Verona	**(Play)** Two Gentlemen of Verona by William Shakespeare
Vagabond King (The)	**(Nov)** If I Were King by Justin Huntly McCarthy
West Side Story	**(Play)** Romeo and Juliet by William Shakespeare
Wicked	**(Nov)** Wicked: The Life and Times of the Wicked Witch of the West by Gregory Maguire
Wiz (The)	**(Nov)** The Wonderful Wizard of Oz by L. Frank Baum
Wizard of Oz (The)	**(Nov)** The Wonderful Wizard of Oz by L. Frank Baum
Woman in White (The)	**(Nov)** The Woman in White by Wilkie Collins
Wonderful Town	**(Play)** My Sister Eileen by Joseph Fields & Jerome Chodorov (and the stories of the same name by Ruth McKenney)
Working	**(Nov)** Working by Studs Terkel
Young Frankenstein	**(Nov)** Frankenstein by Mary Shelley
Zorba	**(Nov)** Zorba the Greek by Nikos Kazantzakis

MUSICALS BASED ON THE BIBLE

Andrew Lloyd Webber and Tim Rice made this type of musical popular. As a result, as well as the commercial musicals, there are now many musicals written which have their roots in Bible stories, but which are primarily for use in schools. They are a splendid way to introduce young people to the joys of musical theatre.

MUSICAL	BIBLE STORY
Godspell	Jesus Christ's last seven days according to the Gospel of St Matthew
Jesus Christ Superstar	Jesus Christ's last seven days through the eyes of Judas Iscariot
Joseph and the Amazing Technicolor Dreamcoat	Joseph, his coat and his dreams

CATALOGUE MUSICALS

This is a relatively new type of musical where the back catalogue of an artist's work is taken and a musical is written around it. This type of musical has the advantage of attracting not only the theatre goer but the fans of the artist in question too.

MUSICAL	CATALOGUE – based on the music of
Buddy	Buddy Holly
Five Guys Named Moe	Featuring Louis Jordan's greatest hits
Mamma Mia	Abba
Never Forget	Take That
Saturday Night Fever	Bee Gees
Tonight's the Night	Rod Stewart
We Will Rock You	Queen

MUSICALS BASED ON FACT

These musicals are based either on true life stories or on real people and, as a result, can often be the most poignant.

MUSICAL	FACT
Annie Get Your Gun	Based on the true story of American sharpshooter Annie Oakley
Barnum	Based on the true story of showman P.T. Barnum
Bernadette	Based on the true story of St Bernadette of Lourdes

MUSICAL	FACT
Best Little Whorehouse in Texas (The)	Based on the true story of a brothel in Texas called the Chicken Ranch
Calamity Jane	Based on the true story of Martha Jane Cannary-Burke
Chicago	Inspired by the true story of the 1924 Chicago housewife Beulah Annan who shot and killed her lover
Evita	Based on the true story of Eva Peron
Fiorello!	Based on the true story of Fiorello LaGuardia, the US Congressman and Mayor of New York
Funny Girl	Based on incidents in the life of Fanny Brice
Gypsy	Based on the true story of Gypsy Rose Lee
I and Albert	Based on Queen Victoria and her husband Prince Albert
Jersey Boys (The)	Based on the true story of Frankie Valli and the Four Seasons
Matchgirls (The)	Based on the 1888 strike by the girls in a match factory.
Mitford Girls (The)	Based on the life of the six Mitford sisters
Parade	Based on the true story of the 1913 trial of Leo Frank
Song of Norway	Based on the life of Edvard Grieg
Sound of Music (The)	Based on the true story of the Von Trapp family
They're Playing Our Song	Based on the partnership of Marvin Hamlisch and Carol Bayer Sager
Tick Tick Boom	Based on the life of the composer Jonathan Larson
Titanic	Based on the sinking of the Titanic

MUSICALS BASED ON FILMS OR TV SHOWS

Musicals in this category have previously been seen in some form or other either on TV (TV) or film (F).

MUSICAL	FILM/TV SHOW
Acorn Antiques	(TV) Acorn Antiques
Applause	(F) All About Eve
Bad Girls – The Musical	(TV) Bad Girls
Big the Musical	(F) Big
Billy Elliot	(F) Billy Elliot
Bugsy Malone	(F) Bugsy Malone
Chitty Chitty Bang Bang	(F) Chitty Chitty Bang Bang
Dale Wasserman	(TV Play) I, Don Quixote
Footloose	(F) Footloose
Full Monty (The)	(F) The Full Monty
Goodbye Girl (The)	(F) The Goodbye Girl
High School Musical	(TVF) High School Musical

MUSICAL	FILM/TV SHOW
Jailhouse Rock	**(F)** Jailhouse Rock
Jerry Springer the Opera	**(TV)** Jerry Springer
King and I (The)	**(F)** Anna and the King of Siam
Legally Blonde	**(F)** Legally Blonde
Lion King (The)	**(F)** The Lion King
Little Mermaid (The)	**(F)** Little Mermaid
A Little Night Music	**(F)** Smiles of a Summer Night
Little Shop of Horrors (The)	**(F)** Little Shop of Horrors
Meet Me in St Louis	**(F)** Meet Me in St Louis
Metropolis	**(F)** Metropolis
My Favourite Year	**(F)** My Favourite Year
Nine	**(F)** 8½
Passion	**(F)** Passione d'Amore
Return to the Forbidden Planet	**(F)** Forbidden Planet (Sci-Fi version of The Tempest)
Saturday Night Fever	**(F)** Saturday Night Fever
Seven Brides for Seven Brothers	**(F)** Seven Brides for Seven Brothers
70 Girls 70	**(F)** Make Mine Mink
Silk Stockings	**(F)** Suggested by the film Ninotchka
Singin' in the Rain	**(F)** Singin' in the Rain
Slipper and the Rose (The)	**(F)** The Slipper and the Rose
Some Like It Hot	**(F)** Some Like It Hot
State Fair	**(F)** State Fair
Sunset Boulevard	**(F)** Sunset Boulevard
Sweet Charity	**(F)** Sweet Charity
Thoroughly Modern Millie	**(F)** Thoroughly Modern Millie
Woman of the Year	**(F)** Woman of the Year
Xanadu	**(F)** Xanadu

MUSICALS FROM 'OTHER' SOURCES

Some musicals derive from sources which will not fit into any of the above categories and yet they are not entirely original.

MUSICAL	MISCELLANEOUS SOURCE
Annie	Inspired by the cartoon strip 'Orphan Annie' in the *Chicago Tribune*
Let's Face It	Based on a newspaper article
Miss Saigon	Inspired by Puccini's *Madame Butterfly* and inspired by a newspaper cutting
Mystery of Edwin Drood (The)	Based on the 'unfinished' novel of the same name by Charles Dickens
Rent	Based on Puccini's *La Bohème*

MUSICAL	MISCELLANEOUS SOURCE
Sally	Based on an unproduced musical *The Little Thing* by P.G. Wodehouse
Snoopy	Based on the comic strip *Peanuts* by Charles M. Schulz

A Short Synopsis of Some of the Most Popular Musicals

ANNIE

Synopsis: It is the 1930s in America and Annie, an orphan, is forced to live an austere and lonely life in an orphanage which is run by a child-hating drunk called Miss Hannigan. On one particular Christmas, she is chosen to spend the festive period with the millionaire Mr Warbucks. This leads to a search for her real parent, who it turns out have died, and her eventual adoption by 'Daddy' Warbucks.

Including the Songs: Annie I Don't Need Anything But You; Easy Street; Hooverville; I Think I'm Gonna Like it Here; It's the Hard Knock Life; Little Girls; Maybe; New Deal for Christmas; NYC; Something was Missing; Tomorrow; You're Never Fully Dressed Without a Smile; You Won't be an Orphan for Long

ANNIE GET YOUR GUN

Synopsis: Sharpshooter Annie Oakley falls in love with her rival, crackshot Frank Butler, and only wins his love when she follows the advice given to her by her friend Chief Sitting Bull. The advice is to deliberately lose a shooting match and let Frank win; so she loses the match and wins the man.

Including the Songs: Anything You Can Do; Colonel Buffalo Bill; Doin' What Comes Naturally; Girl That I Marry (The); I Got Lost in His Arms; I Got the Sun in the Morning; I'm a Bad Bad Man; I'm an Indian Too; Moonshine Lullaby; My Defenses are Down; Old Fashioned Wedding; There's No Business Like Show Business; They Say It's Wonderful; You Can't Get a Man With a Gun

BARNUM

Synopsis: The true story of P.T. Barnum who, from humble beginnings, became 'The Greatest Showman on Earth'.

Including the Songs: Bigger isn't Better; Black and White; Come Follow the Band; Colours of My Life (The); I Like Your Style; Join the Circus; Love

Makes Such Fools of Us All; Museum Song; One Brick at a Time; Out There; Prince of Humbug (The); Thank God I'm Old; There's a Sucker Born Every Minute

BLOOD BROTHERS

Synopsis: The tragic story of Liverpool-born twins who, despite being separated at birth, grow up as close friends totally unaware of their blood relationship; then in a tragic twist of fate one twin kills the other and then he is in turn shot dead by the police.

Including the Songs: Bright New Day; Easy Terms; I'm Not Saying a Word; Light Romance; Long Sunday Afternoon; Madman; Marilyn Monroe; My Child; My Friend; Robbery (The); Shoes Upon the Table; Summer Sequence; Take a Letter Miss Jones; Tell Me It's Not True; That Guy

BOYFRIEND (THE)

Synopsis: Boyfriends are forbidden at Madame Dubonnet's finishing school near Nice in France, but that doesn't stop them! Wealthy Polly Browne, one of the 'young ladies', falls in love with Tony who she believes to be a delivery boy; fortunately for her, he turns out to be the Hon. Tony Brockhurst.

Including the Songs: Boyfriend (The); Fancy Forgetting; I Could Be Happy With You; It's Never too Late to Fall in Love; It's Nicer in Nice; Perfect Young Ladies; Poor Little Pierrette; Riviera (The); Room in Bloomsbury (A); Safety in Numbers; Sur La Plage; Won't You Charleston; You Don't Want to Play with me Blues (The)

BUGSY MALONE

Synopsis: This is a unique 1920s story of gangster warfare in New York, where the gangsters are all played by children and the weapons are splurge guns and old-fashioned custard pies.

Including the Songs: Bugsy Malone; Fat Sam's Grand Slam; I'm Feeling Fine; My Name is Tallulah; Ordinary Fool; Tomorrow; You Give Me a Little Love

CABARET

Synopsis: Set in 1929–1930, on the eve of the Nazi uprising, a young writer falls in love with a cabaret singer, but it is a debauched world in which they live and so their love is doomed from the start with no sign of a happy ending.

Including the Songs: Cabaret; Don't Tell Mama; If You Could See Her; It Couldn't Please Me More; Married; Meeskite; Money Song (The); Perfectly Marvellous; So What?; Telephone Song; Tomorrow Belongs to

Me; Two Ladies; Welcome to the Cabaret (Wilkommen); What Would You Do?; Why Should I Wake Up?

CAROUSEL

Synopsis: Billy Bigelow is a waster but, for once in his life, he gets it right when he falls in love with Julie Jordan. However, things go wrong once again when Julie – now married to Billy – announces that she is pregnant. He can see no way of providing for his family except by taking part in a robbery, during which he dies. After death he is told by the Starmaker that there is no way into heaven unless he does one good deed down on earth to redeem himself and so he returns to help his now 15-year-old daughter, Louise.

Including the Songs: Blow High Blow Low; Geraniums in the Winder; Highest Judge of All (The); If I Loved You; June is Bustin' Out All Over; Mister Snow; My Little Girl; Real Nice Clam Bake (A); Soliloquy (Billy); What's the Use of Wond'rin'; When the Children are Asleep; You'll Never Walk Alone

CATS

Synopsis: This is a dance extravaganza where the action takes place on a huge rubbish dump and where the cats are gathering for the Jellicle Ball. It is at this ball that one cat will be chosen and awarded an extra life. Throughout the events we get to know all the cats and their differing personalities until the final choice is made.

Including the Songs: Addressing of Cats; Awful Battle of the Pekes and Pollicles (The); Ballad of Billy McCaw (The); Bustopher Jones; Grizabella, the Glamour Cat; Growltiger's Last Stand; Gus, the Theatre Cat; Invitation to the Jellicle Ball (The); Jellicle Ball (The); Jellicle Songs for Jellicle Cats; Journey to the Heavy Side Layer (The); Macavity; Marching Song of the Pollicle Dogs (The); Memory; Moments of Happiness (The); Mr Mistoffelees; Mungojerrie and Rumpleteazer; Naming of the Cats (The); Old Deuteronomy; Old Gumbie Cat (The); Rum Tum Tugger; Skimbleshanks

CHICAGO

Synopsis: Set in Cook County Jail, Chicago, in the roaring Twenties, this is the story of murder and corruption where the central figures do not believe they have even committed murder because after all, their men 'had it coming'! Corruption – aided by the lawyer Billy Flynn – wins the day and the two main murderesses win their freedom.

Including the Songs: All That Jazz; All I Care About; Cell Block Tango; Chicago After Midnight; Class; Funny Honey; I Can't Do It Alone; I Know a Girl; Little Bit of Good (A); Me and My Baby; Mister Cellophane; My Own Best Friend; Nowadays; Razzle Dazzle; Roxie; We Both Reached for the Gun; When Velma Takes the Stand; When You're Good to Mama

CHORUS LINE (A)

Synopsis: This has a very simple storyline about a group of dancers auditioning for a part in the ensemble of a musical.

Including the Songs: At the Ballet; Dance Ten Looks Three; Hello Twelve; I Can Do That; I Hope I Get It; Mother; Nothing; One; Sing!

EVITA

Synopsis: This is the true and legendary story of Eva Duarte and her rise from Argentinean poverty to become the wife of Colonel Juan Peron the President of Argentina, making her the First Lady of Argentina and earning her the affectionate name of Evita.

Including the Songs: Actress Hasn't Learned the Lines (The); And the Money Kept Rolling In; A New Argentina; Another Suitcase In Another Hall; Art of the Possible (The); Buenos Aires; Dice Are Rolling; Don't Cry For Me Argentina; Eva Beware of the City; Goodnight and Thank You; High Flying Adored; I'd be Surprisingly Good For You; Lady's Got Potential (The); Lament; Oh What A Circus; On the Balcony of the Casa Rosada; On This Night of a Thousand Stars; Rainbow High; Rainbow Tour; Requiem For Evita; Santa Evita; She is a Diamond; Waltz for Che and Eva

42ND STREET

Synopsis: The story of love and rivalry behind a new Broadway show where the chorus girl triumphs and becomes a star.

Including the Songs: About a Quarter to Nine; Dames; 42nd Street; Getting Out of Town; Go Into Your Dance; I Know Now; Lullaby of Broadway; Pretty Lady Overture; Shadow Waltz; Shuffle off to Buffalo; Sunny Side to Every Situation; We're in the Money; Young and Healthy; You're Getting to be a Habit with Me

FUNNY GIRL

Synopsis: Set around the time of the First World War, *Funny Girl* depicts incidents in the life of Fanny Brice and charts her success as she changes from a typically awkward teenage girl into a national star; it also follows her love story with Nick Arnstein. The real Fanny Brice (1891–1951) was a celebrated American comedienne, actress and singer. She created and starred in the radio comedy show *The Baby Snooks Show*.

Including the Songs: Cornet Man; Don't Rain On My Parade; Find

Yourself a Man; Henry Street; His Love Makes Me Beautiful; If a Girl Isn't Pretty; I'm the Greatest Star; I Want To be Seen With You Tonight; People; Rat-Tat-Tat-Tat (Private Schwartz); Sadie, Sadie (Married Lady); The Music That Makes Me Dance; Who Are You Now?; Who Taught Her Everything?; You Are Woman

GIGI

Synopsis: The scene is the romantic city of Paris at the turn of the Twentieth Century where women were expected to know their place. It is here that her Aunt Alicia is teaching Gigi all the important things she'll need to learn to become the mistress of a wealthy man, such as how to recognise the blue flame at the heart of an emerald and how to choose a cigar for her lover. But this is not what Gigi wants from life. This is a refreshing story of a young girl's determination and strength of character.

Including the Songs: At Maxims – Can-Can; Contract (The); Earth and Other Minor Things (The); Gigi; I'm Glad I'm Not Young Anymore; I Never Want to Go Home Again; In This Wide Wide World; I Remember It Well; It's a Bore; New Dress (The); Night They Invented Champagne (The); Paris is Paris Again; She is Not Thinking of Me; Telephone (The); Thank Heaven for Little Girls

GODSPELL

Synopsis: This is a musical based on the Gospel according to St Matthew, and deals with the last days of Jesus Christ. The approach is unique in that the cast are clowns and they use various styles of interpretation and improvisation.

Including the Songs: Alas for You; All For the Best; All Good Gifts; Bless the Lord; By My Side; Day by Day; Learn Your Lessons Well; Light of the World; On The Willows; Prepare Ye the Way of the Lord; Save the Day; Tower of Babble; Turn Back Oh Man; We Beseech Thee

GUYS AND DOLLS

Synopsis: Sarah Brown is a member of the Save-a-Soul Mission and her one aim in life is to recruit and save sinners. Nathan Detroit, on the other hand, belongs to the gambling fraternity and is only interested in finding a place for his illegal crap game. Nathan and Sky Masterson enter into a bet, the bet being that Sky can take any 'doll' he likes to Havana. Nathan sets him the seemingly insurmountable problem of taking the righteous Sarah Brown. In true Hollywood style, and after numerous problems, the guy gets the gal and everyone lives happily ever after.

Including the Songs: Adelaide's Lament; Bushel and a Peck (A); Crap

Shooters' Ballet; Follow the Fold; Fugue for Tinhorns; Guys and Dolls; Havana Dance; If I Were a Bell; I'll Know; I've Never Been in Love Before; Luck Be a Lady; Marry the Man Today; More I Cannot Wish You; My Time of Day; Oldest Established Crap Game in the World (The); Sit Down, You're Rockin' the Boat; Sue Me; Take Back Your Mink

GYPSY

Synopsis: It is the 1920s and stage struck Mama Rose – the worst stage mother of all time – wants nothing more than for her daughters, Louise and June, to be stars. She pushes June, the more talented of her two girls, until she eventually runs away to marry. It is then that Mama Rose turns her attention to the untalented Louise and, together with Herbie, who is in love with Rose, the three become an act. Herbie accidentally books them into a strip club where on the final night of their stay, the star stripper is arrested and Rose persuades Louise to take her place. Herbie walks out on her in disgust and a star, Gypsy Rose-Lee, is born . . . for this is a true story.

Including the Songs: All I Need is the Girl; Baby June and Her Newsboys; Cow Song; Dainty June and Her Farmboys; Everything's Coming Up Roses; If Momma Was Married; Let Me Entertain You; Little Lamb; Mama Rose's Toreadorables; May We Entertain You; Mr Goldstone I Love You; Rose's Turn; Small World; Some People; Together, Wherever We Go; You Gotta Get a Gimmick; You'll Never Get Away From Me

HALF A SIXPENCE

Synopsis: A poor draper's apprentice, Kipps, is in love with Ann, a servant girl, and gives her half a sixpence as a token of his love, keeping the other half for himself. Shortly afterwards, the pair fall out. Kipps then learns that he has inherited a fortune. However, after many traumas he realises that love has more value than money and he and Ann are reunited.

Including the Songs: Economy; Flash Bang Wallop; Half a Sixpence; I Don't Believe a Word of It; If the Rain's Got to Fall; I Know What I Am; Long Ago; Money to Burn; Old Military Canal (The); One Who's Run Away (The); Party's On the House (The); Proper Gentleman (A); She's Too Far Above Me

HELLO DOLLY

Synopsis: Mrs Dolly Gallagher Levi is a matchmaker, or as she put it in the first scene of the show: 'Some people paint, some sew . . . I meddle.' And so in this show we simply see the results of her meddling!

Including the Songs:
Before the Parade Passes By; Come and be My Butterfly; Dancing; Elegance; Hello Dolly!; It Only Takes a Moment; It Takes a Woman; So

Long Dearie; Love Look in my Window; Motherhood; Put My Hand in; Put On Your Sunday Clothes; Ribbons Down My Back; Waiter's Gallop (The); World Take Me Back

KING AND I (THE)

Synopsis: Set in Bangkok in the early 1860s, *The King and I* tells the story of an English woman, Anna, who is hired as the governess and tutor for the King of Siam's many children. After numerous quarrels, the two fall in love and Anna teaches the King, before his untimely death, how democracy and equality can be good for his country.

Including the Songs: Getting to Know You; Hello Young Lovers; I Whistle a Happy Tune; March of the Siamese Children; My Lord and Master; Puzzlement (A); Shall I Tell You What I think of You; Something Wonderful; We Kiss in a Shadow

KISS ME KATE

Synopsis: This is a play within a play as a once married, now divorced, couple are performing in a musical version of *The Taming of the Shrew*. The pair take their fraught emotions onto the stage with them, threatening the show's success until eventually, in dramatic fashion, all is resolved.

Including the Songs: Always True to You in My Fashion; Another Op'nin', Another Show; Bianca; Brush Up Your Shakespeare; I Am Ashamed That Women are So Simple; I Hate Men; I'm Afraid; I Sing Of Love; I've Come to Live It Wealthily in Padua; Kiss Me Kate; So in Love; Tom, Dick or Harry; Too Darn Hot; We Open in Venice; Were Thine That Special Face; Where is the Life That Late I Led?; Why Can't You Behave?; Wunderbar

LITTLE SHOP OF HORRORS (THE)

Synopsis: A geek by the name of Seymour works in a run-down florist shop where he has a secret crush on another assistant, Audrey. One day, he purchases a strange plant which grows at an alarming rate. The plant brings him fame, fortune and the love of Audrey. However, there is one hitch and that is that the plant is of the man-eating variety and can only thrive by drinking human blood – fresh human blood. It sounds like a horror musical but is actually a comedy and a spoof on the old 'B' movies.

Including the Songs: Call Back in the Morning; Closed for Renovation; Dentist!; Don't it Go to Show Ya Never Know; Git It; Grow for Me; Meek Shall Inherit (The); Mushnik and Son; Now It's Just the Gas; Prologue; Skid Row; Somewhere That's Green; Suddenly Seymour; Suppertime

MACK AND MABEL

Synopsis: This is an unusually dark musical in which, through a series of flashbacks, director Mark Sennet, a hard and aggressive man who is unable to express his true feelings, looks back over his career and the time he discovered the star Mabel Normand, up until her early death from a heroine overdose.

Including the Songs: Big Time; Hundreds of Girls; I Promise You a Happy Ending; I Wanna Make the World Laugh; I Won't Send Roses; Look What Happened to Mabel; Movies were Movies; My Heart Leaps Up; Tap Your Troubles Away; Time Heals Everything; When Mabel Comes into the Room; Wherever He Ain't

MAMMA MIA

Synopsis: Set on a Greek island and based on Abba's music, this tells the story of Sophie who, when planning her marriage to her boyfriend, Sky, realises that she wants her father to give her away. The trouble is, she doesn't know the identity of her real father. Having read her mother's diary she realises that he could be any one of three of them, so she invites all three men to her wedding, which comes as a bit of a shock to her mother!

Including the Songs: Chiquitita; Dancing Queen; Does Your Mother Know; Gimme! Gimme!; Honey, Honey; Knowing Me Knowing You; Lay All Your Love On Me; Mamma Mia; Money, Money, Money; Name of the Game (The); One of Us; Our Last Summer; S.O.S.; Slipping Through My Fingers; Super Trouper; Thank You for the Music; Under Attack; Voulez-Vous

ME AND MY GIRL

Synopsis: A cockney chappie called Bill learns that he is the 14th heir to the Earl of Hareford, but can only inherit the title and money if he is deemed suitable. One thing he is asked to do is to reject his cockney girl-friend, Sally. He refuses to do this and, eventually, Sally learns how to be a lady.

Including the Songs:
An English Gentlemen; Family Solicitor (The); If Only You Had Cared for Me; Lambeth Walk (The); Leaning On a Lamp Post; Love Makes the World Go Round; Me and My Girl; Once You Lose Your Heart; Song of Hareford; Take It On the Chin; Sun Has Got His Hat On (The); Thinking of No-one But Me; Weekend at Hareford is Simply Divine (A); You Would If You Could

OKLAHOMA!

Synopsis: The musical is set in Indian territory in America at the turn of the century. It is not only the Indians who are a problem, but also the farmers and the cowmen who have a deep seated mistrust of each other; add to that the usual mix of boy wants girl, can't get girl, but ends up with girl, and you have a typical happy musical.

Including the Songs: All Er Nothin'; Farmer and the Cowman (The); I Cain't Say No; It's a Scandal It's an Outrage; Kansas City; Lonely Room; Many a New Day; Oh, What a Beautiful Morning; Oklahoma!; People Will Say We're in Love; Por Jud is Daid; Surrey With the Fringe on Top (The)

PAJAMA GAME (THE)

Synopsis: This is a story about trade unions with a cast of factory hands, office workers and shop stewards; a strike is imminent and so is love between Sid and Babe, who are on the two opposing sides. Eventually, the dispute is resolved and love is allowed to flourish.

Including the Songs: Her Is; Hernando's Hideaway; Hey There; I'll Never Be Jealous Again; I'm Not at All in Love; New Town is a Blue Town (A); Pajama Game (The); Racing with the Clock; Seven and a Half Cents; Sleep Tite; Small Talk; Steam Heat; There Once Was a Man; Think of the Time I Save; Year Day (A)

PHANTOM OF THE OPERA (THE)

Synopsis: The Paris Opera House is reputedly haunted and when a curtain falls, almost killing the Prima Donna, Carlotta, she refuses to go on stage and is replaced by Christine, who has been having singing lessons from a mysterious teacher, Angel of Music – the Phantom. Christine is in love with Raoul but is told by the madly jealous Phantom that if she does not stay with him in the bowels of the Opera House then Raoul will die.

Including the Songs: Angel of Music; Down One More/Track Down This; I Remember/Stranger Than You Dreamt It; Little Lotte/The Mirror (Angel of Music); Magical Lasso; Masquerade; Murderer; Music of the Night; Notes/Prima Donna; Phantom of the Opera (The); Point of No Return (The); Poor Fool He Makes Me Laugh; Think of Me; Twisted Every Way; Wandering Child/Bravo; Why Have You Brought Me Here/All I Ask of You; Wishing You Were Somehow Here Again

RENT

Synopsis: Based on Puccini's *La Bohème*, *Rent* takes a look at the different pressures and problems today's youth face.

Including the Songs: Another Day; Christmas Bells; Contact; Finale;

Goodbye Love; Halloween; Happy New Year; I'll Cover You; I'll Cover You – Reprise; I Should Tell You; La Vie Bohème; Life Support; Light My Candle; On the Street; One Song Glory; Out Tonight; Over the Moon; Rent; Santa Fe; Seasons of Love; Take Me or Leave Me; Tango: Maureen; Today 4 U; Tune Up # 1, 2, 3; Voice Mail # 1, 2, 3, 4, 5; We're Okay; What You Own; Will I; Without You; You Okay, Honey?; You'll See; Your Eyes

RETURN TO THE FORBIDDEN PLANET

Synopsis: A musical based on the sci-fi film *Forbidden Planet* which, in turn, was based on Shakespeare's *The Tempest*. One night, a mad scientist works on a formula to change the world, but it changes more than expected, resulting in far-reaching consequences. The music isn't original, but well-known popular classics are used.

Including the Songs: Ain't Gonna Wash for a Week; All Shook Up; Born to be Wild; Don't Let Me be Misunderstood; Gloria; Good Vibrations; Great Balls of Fire; Hey, Mr Spaceman; It's a Man's World; Monster Mash; Only the Lonely; Robot Man; Shake, Rattle and Roll; She's Not There; Teenager in Love; Tell Her; Who's Sorry Now?; Wipe Out; Young Girl

SEVEN BRIDES FOR SEVEN BROTHERS

Synopsis: Adam goes into town to find himself a bride and, in a far-fetched whirlwind romance, marries Molly who then believes that she is heading for an idyllic life in the country. When she reaches her new home, she finds Adam's six brothers living in total squalor and sets about on a mission to teach them the social niceties of life. With their new manners and clean clothes, the brothers make an impression on the local girls, who they then kidnap in an attempt to get themselves a wife, as their elder brother had done before them. Fortunately, each of the girls falls in love with and marries her respective kidnapper.

Including the Songs: Bless Your Beautiful Hide; Glad You Were Born; Goin' Courtin'; June Bride; Lonesome Polecat; Love Never Goes Away; One Man; Sobbin' Women; Social Dance; Spring Dance; Townsfolk Lament (The); We've Gotta Make It Through the Winter; Woman Ought to Know Her Place (A); Wonderful Wonderful Day

SINGIN' IN THE RAIN

Synopsis: It is the 1920s and silent movies are giving way to talkies. The change over from silence to sound uncovers other problems – that some of the stars can't actually speak! This is a feel good extravaganza epitomising the Hollywood musical.

Including the Songs: All I Do is Dream of You; Beautiful Girl; Broadway Melody; Fit as a Fiddle; Good Morning; Make 'Em Laugh; Moses Supposes;

Singin' in the Rain; What's Wrong with Me?; Would You; You Stepped Out of a Dream; You Were Meant for Me

SUNSET BOULEVARD
Synopsis: Joe Gillis is a young and struggling screenwriter who agrees to help Norma Desmond finish her own screenplay which she hopes will help her make a comeback and relaunch her fading career. Norma falls in love with Joe and is insanely jealous when she discovers that he is having an affair with Betty Schaefer, another young screenwriter. Added to that is the fact that no one is interested in her comeback and so, finally, she loses her grip on reality, with tragic results.
Including the Songs:
As If We Never Said Goodbye; Back at the House On Sunset; Eternal Youth is Worth a Little Suffering; Every Movie's a Circus; Girl Meets Boy; Greatest Star of All (The); Lady's Paying (The); Let's Have Lunch; New Ways to Dream; Perfect Year (The); Phone Call; Prologue; Salome; Sunset Boulevard; Surrender; There's Been a Call; This Time Next Year; Too Much in Love to Care; Who's Betty Schaefer; With One Look

SWEET CHARITY
Synopsis: Misfortune and chaos seem to follow the naïve and gullible Charity Agnes Valentine around as she lurches from one drama to another.
Including the Songs: Baby, Dream Your Dream; Big Spender; Charity's Soliloquy; If My Friends Could See Me Now; I Love to Cry at Weddings; I'm a Brass Band; I'm the Bravest Individual; Rhythm of Life (The); Rich Man's Frug (dance); Sweet Charity; There's Gotta Be Something Better Than This; Too Many Tomorrows; Where Am I Going?; You Should See Yourself

WEST SIDE STORY
Synopsis: A classic musical loved the world over, this story of doomed love is based on William Shakespeare's *Romeo and Juliet*. It is set in the slums of New York where two young people from opposing 'gangs' – the Sharks and the Jets – fall in love, ensuring a tragic ending instead of the usual 'happy ever after' conclusion expected of musicals.
Including the Songs: America; Cool; Boy Like That (A); Dance at the Gym; Gee Officer Krupke; I Feel Pretty; I Have a Love; Jet Song; Maria; One Hand One Heart; Rumble (The); Something's Coming; Tonight

WE WILL ROCK YOU
Synopsis: It is way into the future where music has been banned and everyone lives in a perfect cloned world. A group of young people are

not happy with this way of life and search for real music and instruments; this is a feel-good musical based on the music of rock legends Queen. **Including the Songs:** Another One Bites the Dust; Bohemian Rhapsody; Crazy Little Thing Called Love; Don't Stop Me Now; Headlong; I Want it All; I Want to Break Free; Innuendo; Killer Queen; Kind of Magic (A); No One But You; One Vision; Play the Game; Radio Ga Ga; Seven Seas of Rye; Somebody to Love; These are the Days of Our Life; Under Pressure; We are the Champions; We Will Rock You; Who Wants to Live Forever

A Brief Storyline of Other Musicals

I have given you a brief synopsis of some of the more well-known musicals, but often someone will ask me for the basic storyline of the lesser known musicals. Here you will find it, a very brief and very basic storyline.

MUSICAL	BASIC STORYLINE
A	
Acorn Antiques	The principals from the axed TV show have been reunited to turn the soap into a musical.
Act (The)	The story of Michelle Craig's nightclub act and her subsequent memories.
Aida	A flashback to ancient Egypt which tells the story of a love triangle.
Allegro	Portrays one man's life from his birth in 1905 until his 35th year.
Anyone Can Whistle	An unconventional satire on society as various characters fight to save a bankrupt town.
Anything Goes	A stowaway on board a ship tries to win the heart of the woman he loves.
Applause	A musical about show business and what all performers want from it – applause.
Aspects of Love	A show depicting, as the title suggests, all the complexities of love.
Assassins	A musical which looks at the history of Presidential assassinations in America.
Avenue Q	A mix of puppets and 'real' people tell the comedic story of a college graduate's journey of self-discovery.
B	
Babes in Arms	A group of young apprentices put on a show to raise money for the theatre's kindly owner.

MUSICAL	BASIC STORYLINE
Baby	The story of three couples, each expecting a child, and their very different reactions.
Bad Girls the Musical	Life in a women's prison based on the original TV series of the same name.
Baker's Wife (The)	The story of the baker's wife, the chauffeur and the baker, who refuses to sell his bread until she returns to him.
Bat Boy	Some teenagers discover a pointy-eared child in a cave and take him back to their town.
Beautiful Game (The)	The story of ordinary teenage boys and their love of football and girls.
Bells are Ringing (The)	The story revolves around a telephone answering service, which the police think is a vice ring.
Bernadette	The true story of a little French peasant girl who claimed to have seen visions of a 'beautiful lady' – the Virgin Mary.
Best Little Whorehouse in Texas (The)	Based on the true story of a brothel which, having survived for years, is suddenly put under scrutiny.
Big River	Adventure loving Huckleberry Finn runs away from his alcoholic father and, as usual, has adventures on the way.
Big the Musical	A young boy's wish to be an adult is granted, but it is not all he expected, based on the film *Big*.
Billy	Billy, a working-class boy creates a fantasy life to escape from what he sees as his own humdrum life.
Billy Elliot	A young working-class boy makes it in the world of dance.
Bitter Sweet	A woman looks back at her life and knows that she never stopped loving her first love – her singing teacher.
Bless the Bride	Lucy is about to marry the Hon. Thomas Trout when she leaves him at the church to elope with a Frenchman, Pierre Fontaine. The couple travel to France where they get separated but are later reunited and marry.
Blitz	A look at how a family survives the war and their own personal traumas.
Blondel	The story of a minstrel's devotion to Richard the Lionheart.
Bombay Dreams	A poor young man dreams of becoming a movie star when fate takes a hand and he meets the daughter of a Bollywood film director. Will this help him?
Bounce	The story of American men and women who are prepared to take risks to achieve their dream.
Boys From Syracuse (The)	Twins and mistaken identities abound.
Brigadoon	Brigadoon is village which comes to life for only one day every hundred years, and to fall in love with someone on that day in that village is not without its problems.
Buddy	The story of Buddy Holly's life and music.
Budgie	Set in the sleazy world of Soho with more undesirable characters and encounters than one could imagine rolled into one plot.

MUSICAL	BASIC STORYLINE
Bye Bye Birdie	Rock and Roll superstar Conrad Birdie is about to be drafted into the army, but before then, he must kiss a lucky girl on the Ed Sullivan show.
By Jeeves	A show within a show – and a missing banjo.

C

Calamity Jane	Crackshot Calamity Jane starts to behave like a woman – almost – and wins the love of a man.
Call Me Madam	Sally Adams becomes US Ambassador to the tiny duchy of Lichtenburg, where romance abounds despite objections from Washington.
Camelot	The story of King Arthur's wife, Guinevere and his friend, Sir Lancelot.
Can Can	Judge Aristide wants to close down La Mome Pistache's Dance Hall but, instead, falls in love with her and helps her to save it.
Candide	This is a satirical send-up of optimistic philosophies.
Canterbury Tales	A group of pilgrims tell tales as they journey to Canterbury.
Card (The)	The story of a pushy, opportunist and how he gets what he wants.
Caroline or Change	A story of race and human rights set just after J.F. Kennedy's assassination.
Carrie	The story of an awkward teenage girl whose life is dominated by her religious mother and how she wreaks havoc on everyone and everything.
Charlie Girl	An aristocrat opens her home to aid finances; an employer falls in love with her youngest daughter and then he wins a fortune!
Chess	A metaphorical look at romance and the East-West problem through the game of chess.
Children of Eden	Based freely on the stories of Adam, Eve, Noah, their children and their 'Father', it looks at the difficulty of parenting.
Chitty Chitty Bang Bang	The story of an eccentric inventor, his children, a magical car and an evil baron who wants the car.
City of Angels	It is 1940s Hollywood and novelist, Stine, is attempting to write a screenplay when the characters in his imagination come to life on stage.
Closer to Heaven	Set in London's clubland with stories of homosexuality and drugs.
Coco	The life of the designer Coco Channel.
Color Purple (The)	The story of how one woman proves that love does conquer all.
Company	A bachelor looks at the lives of his married friends and decides that there is 'no point to life' without someone to share it with.

MUSICAL	BASIC STORYLINE
Connecticut Yankee	Martin is knocked out and has a vivid dream through which he realises exactly who is the love of his life.
Contact	Three dance pieces in one show, which are set to pre-recorded classical and popular recordings. There is virtually no book, no orchestra and no live singing.
Copacabana	An aspiring songwriter hopes to create the next hit when his imagination takes him back to the 1940s and he creates a story around a young singer called Lola.
Crazy for You	Instead of closing down a theatre, as he is supposed to do, a stage-struck playboy, Bobby Child, falls in love with the theatre owner's daughter, Polly, and then raises money to save the theatre.
Curtains	During the curtain call of a bad show, the leading lady is murdered and the race is on to find the killer and salvage the show.

D

Daddy Cool	The story of a young man who lives for his music, a difficult love and rival gangs.
Dames at Sea	This is a spoof of the 1930s-style Busby Berkeley film musical in which an understudy steps into a role and becomes a star.
Damn Yankees	Joe agrees to sell his soul to the devil in order to save his favourite team, but he eventually manages to outwit the devil.
Dancing Years (The)	The story of a penniless composer and his love for two entirely different women – one an innkeeper's daughter, the other an opera singer.
Desert Song (The)	General Birabeau is sent to capture the Red Shadow bandit who, it turns out, is more gentleman than bandit.
Doctor Dolittle	The story of a man who can talk to animals.
Dreamgirls	Three talented black, female singers called the Dreamettes rename themselves 'The Dreams', not realising how hard the world of showbiz really is.

E

Expresso Bongo	The story of one young man's unscrupulous rise to fame.

F

Fame	This follows some students through their four-year course at the New York School of Performing Arts.
Fantasticks	Two fathers attempt to manage their children.
Fiddler On the Roof	Tevye's three daughters refuse to stick with tradition and marry the men chosen by him and the matchmaker.
Fifty Million Frenchmen	A young American millionaire bets his friend that he can live without his money for a month.

MUSICAL	BASIC STORYLINE
Fings Ain't Wot They Used T'Be	A down-at-heal gangster tries to make a comeback and ends up going straight, and the bobby on the beat turns to crime.
Finian's Rainbow	A political satire involving a pot of gold, a leprechaun and a racist bigot.
Fiorello!	The story of a good guy coming to power in the US – and falling in love!
Five Guys Named Moe	A revue which focuses more on the songs than the plot!
Fix (The)	A well-liked presidential candidate is dead and so his power-mad widow pushes her son into the political arena.
Flora the Red Menace	A group of people try to find work in the Depression.
Flower Drum Song	A comedy dealing with the generation gap between the old traditional Chinese generation and the New World Chinese.
Follies	Two middle-aged people meet at a reunion and rekindle their feelings but, at the end of the evening, return to their own partners.
Footloose	One young man's fight to have dancing reinstated in a town where it has been banned.
Full Monty (The)	Six unemployed, impoverished steelworkers become a team of male strippers to earn some money.
Funny Thing Happened On the Way to the Forum (A)	A farce in which a slave attempts to win his freedom by helping his master to win the woman he loves.

G

Gay Divorce	Mimi wants a divorce and so a professional co-respondent is hired. The problem is, Mimi mistakes someone else for this person! Note, the American film version is called *The Gay Divorcee*.
Gone with the Wind	The American Civil War begins and so does the love story to end all love stories – that of Scarlett O'Hara and Rhett Butler.
Goodbye Girl (The)	Boyfriends come and go and Lucy is afraid that the latest love in her mother's life will be like all the others and say goodbye in the end.
Grand Hotel	The centre of the action is the Grand Hotel and its eccentric guests.
Grease	Typical boy meets girl, boy gets girl love story set in an American High School.

H

Hair	A 1960s rock musical where love rules and anything goes.
Hairspray	The story of a large girl who only wants to dance and how she wins a part on a TV show and then sets out to win her man and stamp out racism.

85

MUSICAL	BASIC STORYLINE
High School Musical	A sort of modern day Romeo and Juliet, this is the story of two young people, Troy and Gabriella, who despite their different lifestyles, are brought together by their love of singing. They meet during the vacation and when school begins Troy finds that Gabriella is a new girl at his school. Together they decide to audition for the High School Musical. However, this is a plan that is not encouraged or liked by some of the other students which causes problems.
Hallelujah Baby	Georgina wants to be on the stage, but this is America when blacks and whites don't mix and Georgina is black.
High Society	Tracy is about to marry her second husband, George, amid media interest with a male and female reporter covering the story. The male reporter falls in love with Tracy and the female reporter with George.
Hired Man (The)	A look at family life in the early Twentieth Century through the eyes of one family.
Honk!	An updated version of Hans Christian Andersen's tale of The Ugly Duckling.
Hot Mikado	A 1940s style version of the original *Mikado* by W.S. Gilbert and Arthur Sullivan.
How to Succeed in Business Without Really Trying	The story of a young man who, with his girl by his side, uses just a book of simple instructions to get to the top of the business tree.

♪

I Love You, You're Perfect, Now Change	A candid insight into dating, romance, marriage, lovers, husbands, wives and in-laws.
Into the Woods	A story with a moral told through various fairy tales, with the central story being of a childless couple.

♫

Jailhouse Rock	Whilst in jail, Vince Everett discovers that he has a special talent for singing and, upon his release, he becomes a world famous rock star.
Jekyll and Hyde	In an experiment, one man becomes the two personalities of good and evil.
Jerry Springer the Opera	Based on the outrageous TV show – this is even more outrageous.
Jersey Boys	The rags-to-riches story of Frankie Valli and the Four Seasons.
Jesus Christ Superstar	The story of the last seven days in the life of Christ seen through the eyes of Judas.
Joseph and the Amazing Technicolor Dreamcoat	Based on the Bible story of Joseph, his coat and his dreams.
Jubilee	Faced with an impending revolution, a fictional royal family of a fictional country abandon their responsibilities in order to pursue their own dreams.

MUSICAL	BASIC STORYLINE
Just So	Based on the stories Rudyard Kipling repeatedly used to tell his daughter who insisted that they never change and remained 'Just So'!

K

King's Rhapsody	The story of a king, his mistress and a wife he truly loves.
Kismet	The story of a street poet in Baghdad and how he comes across a fortune, buys girls, bids for a palace, gets himself arrested, involved in murder – and love!
Kiss of the Spiderwoman	Two prisoners fall in love when in a dismal South American prison; their relationship eventually leads to the death of one.

L

La Cage aux Folles	A gay couple's life is thrown into turmoil when the son of one – the result of a heterosexual fling – brings home a girl whose father is an influential bigot.
La Cava	This story, which is set in Spain and Morocco in the Eighth Century, is based on the legend of the King of Spain's infatuation with a beautiful young girl.
Lady be Good	A brother and sister are down on their luck and sing and dance at the homes of the wealthy, before coming into money.
Lady in the Dark	A fashion magazine editor tries psycho-analysis to conquer her insecurities – all the numbers are sung during the dream sequences she describes to her doctor.
Last Five Years (The)	A look at the five-year-life of a marriage from the man's point of view in forward time and from the woman's point of view in reverse time.
Leave It to Me	A satire on Communism and US diplomacy.
Legally Blonde	A young girl gets herself into an Ivy League university in order to impress and win back the love of her life.
Les Misérables	An epic musical dealing with a student uprising in France and the social difficulties of the time.
Lestat	A story of vampires.
Let 'Em Eat Cake	A sequel to *Of Thee I Sing* and a political spoof on a Fascist America in which the women of America unite, ensuring a happy ending prevails.
Let's Face It	Suspicious wives try to trap what they believe to be their erring husbands.
Life (The)	It's the 1980s and life on the Times Square streets is colourful – to say the least.
Lion King (The)	A young lion cub grows up and learns about the circle of life.
Little Me	A Hollywood glamour queen dreams of romance with the richest kid from another walk of life.
Little Mermaid (The)	Based on the Disney film of the same name.

MUSICAL	BASIC STORYLINE
Little Night Music (A)	Looks at the complex love lives of several couples.
Lord of the Rings	Tolkien's epic story of good, evil and magic is told in spectacular Cirque du Soleil style.

M

Mame	Orphan Patrick Dennis goes to live with his Aunt Mame, a wild party animal, until she loses her money. Eventually, she marries a rich man who later dies and she spends her money on a home for single mothers.
Man of La Mancha	Based on *The Adventures of Don Quixote* and the struggle to make the world a better place in which to live.
Martin Guerre	Believing that his best friend Martin is dead, Arnaud goes to inform Martin's wife. The two then fall in love, but Martin is not dead and returns to his wife.
Mary Poppins	A magical nanny brings two naughty children into line.
Matchgirls (The)	The girls in a match factory strike against their appalling working conditions.
Merrily We Roll Along	An unusual structure where the musical moves backwards in time to explain how the lead character has become the man he is today.
Merry Widow (The)	She is a wealthy widow, so he won't propose in case she thinks he wants her money.
Metropolis	There are those who live in luxury above ground and those who work underground providing for the elitists above.
Miss Saigon	Chris fathers a Vietnamese child during the war but now has a new American wife. He goes back to see his son, whose mother kills herself, leaving Chris to care for his child.
Moby Dick	The girls of St Godley's School perform *Moby Dick the Musical* to raise funds for their doomed school.
Mr Cinders	A different take on the traditional fairy tale, Cinderella.
Music in the Air	The story of putting on a show, where the lesson to be learnt is that the theatre is no place for amateurs.
Music Man (The)	A con man plans to make money by selling 'instruments' to a boy band and then run away with the money. However, he falls in love with the piano teacher and forsakes his plans.
My Fair Lady	An East End girl learns how to become a lady and falls in love with her teacher on the way.
My Favourite Year	In this farce, a young, naïve TV writer must keep a hard drinking star sober for his guest appearance on a TV show.
My One and Only	Captain Billy Buck Chandler, an aviator, flies around the world in pursuit of the girl he loves. She, meanwhile, is being blackmailed, but Billy rescues her.
Mystery of Edwin Drood (The)	A musical whodunit in which the audience vote for whomever they think committed the murder.

MUSICAL	BASIC STORYLINE

N

Never Forget
A comedy about a Take That tribute band as they learn through pretending to be someone they're not.

Nine
A disturbing incident at the age of nine still influences and affects a film director's life.

No, No, Nanette
Too much money and suspicions about affairs which are not happening cause problems all round.

No Strings
Barbara, a model living in Paris, falls in love with David, a writer suffering from writers' block. Realising that he can only work in America he asks Barbara to go with him, but she refuses.

Notre Dame de Paris
Social outcast Quasimodo loves the beautiful gypsy girl, Esmeralda. It is a love, however, doomed to end in tragedy and death for both.

O

Of Thee I Sing
A political satire based on the election campaign and Presidency of John P. Wintergreen, who promises that, if elected, he will marry a girl chosen for him in a beauty pageant.

Oh, Kay!
It's Prohibition and there is hidden booze, accidental bigamy, and a butler who is not really a butler, in this fun story.

Oliver!
Based on a Dickens tale, after a lot of unhappiness a young orphan finds that he does have a family after all.

Once On this Island
A peasant girl falls in love with a rich city boy.

On the Town
Three sailors are on 24-hour leave from their ship and spend the time in New York City where they meet various women.

On Your Toes
A music teacher tries to persuade the director of the Russian Ballet to stage his friend's jazz ballet; disaster follows.

P

Pacific Overtures
Japan had lived in peace until the culture clash in 1853, when the Americans arrived to open up Japan to the West.

Pal Joey
Joey treats his girlfriend, Linda, badly and has an affair with wealthy, married Vera. Vera then helps Joey to start his own nightclub. Eventually, Linda and Vera join forces to run Joey out of town.

Parade
The true story of a man accused of the rape and murder of a 13-year-old girl. His sentence was reduced due to problems with the trial, but a lynching party hanged him anyway.

Passion
There are two women in Giorgio's life, his mistress Clara who is married and Fosca who is ill. His mistress decides to stay with her husband and Fosca dies, leaving Giorgio alone.

MUSICAL	BASIC STORYLINE
Perchance to Dream	This musical travels through different periods in time telling the parallel and interconnecting stories of various inhabitants of the same house.
Pickwick	A farce which revolves around Mr Samuel Pickwick and Sam Weller as they reminisce about how they ended up in a debtors' prison.
Pipe Dream	Life is hard on Cannery Row where all the loners and runaways search for their dreams.
Pippin	Prince Pippin sought his happiness in the tangible and material things, but eventually found true happiness in home and family.
Pirate Queen (The)	Grace O'Malley, a pirate and mother who lived in Sixteenth Century Ireland, sets sail to confront her rival, Queen Elizabeth I, and protect her people.
Porgy and Bess	In an African-American tenement, life is hard when Crown, a tough labourer, murders Robbins. He leaves town and Bess, Crown's girlfriend, goes to Porgy, a cripple. When Crown returns, Porgy kills him so he can keep Bess.
Producers (The)	A Broadway producer and a young accountant plan to raise thousands of dollars from backers, put on a flop show and abscond with the leftover money – but the show is a hit!

R

Rags	It's the turn of the century and a Russian-Jewish immigrant to the USA is shocked to find that her husband is becoming Americanised in order to climb the social ladder.
Ragtime	The story of American life at the beginning of the Nineteenth Century, focusing on social issues of the period, such as immigration and racism.
Ragged Child (The)	A 'social musical' and ideal for use in schools, this is a moving story of child deprivation in the mid-1800s and the founding of the Ragged Schools.
Rink (The)	Anna's roller rink is about to be demolished and so becomes an extra arena in which mother and daughter examine their past, present and future.
Roar of the Greasepaint – The Smell of the Crowd	Not a musical in the traditional sense, but a look at the game of life where one man always plays by the rules while the other always ignores them.
Robert and Elizabeth	Elizabeth, a poet, is ruled by her tyrannical father and believes herself to be sick; she is freed from her father and her sickroom by the love of Robert, another poet. Based on the Barrett Browning love story.
Rocky Horror Picture Show (The)	A young couple's car breaks down and they find themselves taking refuge in a bizarre castle with even more bizarre inhabitants, the result being orgies, murder and confusion.

MUSICAL	BASIC STORYLINE

S

Salad Days
The story of a piano which, when played, incites all within earshot to dance.

Sally
A typical rags to riches story where Sally – a dishwasher – poses as a famous ballerina finding both fame and love.

Saturday Night Fever
A young man, Tony Manero, escapes his humdrum life and dead end job by disco dancing away each weekend.

Scarlet Pimpernel (The)
It is the time of the French Revolution and the Scarlet Pimpernel tries to save any possible victim of the guillotine.

Scrooge
Based on Charles Dickens' novel *A Christmas Carol*, this tells us the story of how the visitation of three ghosts changes the nature of Ebenezer Scrooge for ever.

Secret Garden (The)
A young, rich, spoilt child changes the lives of a family when she discovers a secret garden and introduces happiness where there was pain.

Seesaw
A man and a woman from totally opposite backgrounds meet and, as a consequence, learn a lot about themselves.

1776
It is a changing world as America struggles for independence from the British.

70 Girls 70
A group of pensioners turn to crime to save their home from closure.

She Loves Me
A secret pen-pal relationship blossoms into a love affair.

Show Boat
A story which is set on an American river boat and focuses on the wrongs of racism.

Silk Stockings
Nina Yaschenko is sent by the Soviet Union to rescue three foolish Commissars who are finding life in the West too attractive.

Snoopy
Snoopy the beagle has style, and is possibly a bit of a social snob too; he is also unrecognised by the human race.

Some Like It Hot
Two out of work musicians witness a gangland killing and so become the next targets. To escape, they dress as women and join an all-girl band.

Song of Norway
Based on the life of Edvard Grieg and telling the story of his love for his childhood sweetheart and his country.

Songs For a New World
A collection of Jason Robert Brown songs where the cohesive theme is decision.

Sound of Music (The)
A novice nun acts as a governess to seven motherless children and falls in love with their widowered father.

South Pacific
Set against a US army base in the South Pacific during the Second World War as they are, love stories can never hope to be easy or even safe from death.

Spamalot
Supposedly the story of King Arthur's quest to find the Holy Grail. However, any hope of sticking rigidly to the plot is lost when one remembers its base is Monty Python!

MUSICAL	BASIC STORYLINE
Spend Spend Spend	Based on the true story of Viv Nicholson who won a fortune on the football pools. When asked what she was going to do with it, she said, 'Spend, spend, spend.'
Spring Awakening	It is the Nineteenth Century where sex is taboo, but that doesn't halt the sexual awakening in two young people.
Starlight Express	Steam versus electric as the trains race – on roller-skates.
State Fair	Set in America where a family enjoy the fun of the annual State Fair.
Stepping Out	A group of women and one man attend a weekly tap class where, as well as tap, they learn a lot more.
Stop the World – I Want to Get Off	The story of a man who becomes a father too early in life, achieves business success and yet still fails to recognise the wealth he has in his wife's true love.
Strike Up the Band	Set almost entirely in a dream, it deals with a war between the US and Switzerland over the tariffs on imported chocolate.
Sunday in the Park with George	It is Nineteenth Century France; George is obsessed with his art and not his pregnant girlfriend, Dot, so she leaves him. Time moves to Twentieth Century America where George's great-grandson is struggling with his art and is helped by Dot's spirit.
Sunny	To avoid an unwanted marriage, Sunny stows aboard a ship bound for New York but, to disembark, she has to marry Jim, though she loves Tom. She divorces Jim and then realises that she did love him and so they remarry.
Sweeney Todd	Sweeney Todd seeks revenge for false imprisonment by going on a murderous rampage. The bodies of his victims are unknowingly cooked in pies by Mrs Lovett, from whom he rents a room.

𝒯

25th Annual Putnam County Spelling Bee	Not only do the contestants compete against each other in this Bee, but they compete against the audience too.
Taboo	Traditional boy meets girl love story set against a backdrop of the gay club scene.
Tell Me On a Sunday	A one-woman show telling the story of a single girl in New York.
They're Playing Our Song	A story based on the real-life relationship between Marvin Hamlisch and Carol Bayer-Sager, which starts as a working relationship and evolves into love.
Thoroughly Modern Millie	A young girl moves to the fast-changing city in search of a new life for herself.
Tick Tick Boom	An autobiographical look at composer, Jonathan Larson's own struggle to write a successful musical.
Time	A Time Lord has to decide whether the 'earth people' are a threat to universal peace.

MUSICAL	BASIC STORYLINE
Titanic	A musical dramatisation of the sinking of the Titanic.
Tommy	A young deaf, dumb and blind boy discovers he has an exceptional talent on the pinball machine and becomes an international superstar. The Who's cult movie.
Two Gentlemen of Verona	A multi-racial rock version of Shakespeare's classic comedy where lifelong friends become rivals in love.

V

Vagabond King (The)	It is Paris and a villain boasts that he can do a better job than the current King. He is then made King for the day and told that, if he fails to do just that, then he will hang.

W

We Will Rock You	Set in the future where music is banned. A group of bohemians go in search of instruments to reinstate real live music.
Wicked	In the city of Oz lives green-skinned Elphaba the misunderstood and her beautiful friend Glinda. The animals are under threat and Elphaba tries to protect them, but all does not turn out well for her.
Wild Party (The)	It is the 1920s when Queenie and Burrs throw the party of the decade to help their shaky relationship, a party which ends in death and destruction.
Will Rogers Follies	Based on the life of Will Rogers, a humourist and performer, where all the major events in his life are portrayed as big production numbers.
Witches of Eastwick	Three modern-day witches innocently wish for the perfect man, and then he arrives to wreak havoc.
Wiz (The)	A modern-inspired version of the perennial Wizard of Oz.
Wizard of Oz (The) (stage Version)	A young girl dreams of a magical land.
Woman in White (The)	Evil Sir Percival Glyde plots to take Marian Halcombe and her younger half-sister, Laura Fairlie's wealth, but a mysterious, ghost-like woman in white, Anne Catherick, tries to help.
Woman of the Year	The pressures of being named as Woman of the Year prove to be too much for Tess Harding and she loses the man she loves.
Wonderful Town	The adventures of two women who travel to New York to make their fortunes.
Working	A look at the different lives of various 'ordinary' working folk.

X

Xanadu	The nine Muses from Ancient Greece come to life on a Venice Beach wall mural.

MUSICAL	BASIC STORYLINE
𝒴	
Young Frankenstein	A funny twist on Mary Shelley's classic tale of Frankenstein.
𝟤	
Zorba	The story follows Zorba, his friend Nikos, their romantic associations and the ensuing tragedies.

Matching Songs to Musicals

Sometimes we find ourselves singing a song and yet we cannot pinpoint the actual musical from which it originated. Here is a list of songs you are most likely to find yourself singing in the shower, together with their musical.

TITLE OF SONG	MUSICAL
All That Jazz	*Chicago*
Almost Like Being in Love	*Brigadoon*
Always True to You in My Fashion	*Kiss Me Kate*
Another Op'nin', Another Show	*Kiss Me Kate*
Anything You Can Do	*Annie Get Your Gun*
Aquarius	*Hair*
Bad Guys	*Bugsy Malone*
Bewitched, Bothered & Bewildered	*Pal Joey*
Big Spender	*Sweet Charity*
Bigger Isn't Better	*Barnum*
Bless Your Beautiful Hide	*Seven Brides for Seven Brothers*
Brush Up Your Shakespeare	*Kiss Me Kate*
Can You Feel the Love Tonight?	*The Lion King*
Cheek to Cheek	*Top Hat*
Cockeyed Optimist	*South Pacific*
Come Follow the Band	*Barnum*
Day by Day	*Godspell*
Diamonds are a Girl's Best Friend	*Gentlemen Prefer Blondes*
Did You Evah?	*High Society*
Doin' What Comes Naturally	*Annie Get Your Gun*
Don't Rain on My Parade	*Funny Girl*
Don't Tell Mamma	*Cabaret*
Ease on Down the Road	*The Wiz*
Everything's Coming Up Roses	*Gypsy*
Feed the Birds	*Mary Poppins*

TITLE OF SONG	MUSICAL
Fit as a Fiddle	Singin' in the Rain
Flash Bang Wallop	Half a Sixpence
Friendship	Anything Goes
Getting to Know You	The King and I
Gonna Build a Mountain	Stop the World – I Want to Get Off
Good Morning	Singin' in the Rain
Happy Talk	South Pacific
Heaven Help My Heart	Chess
Hello Young Lovers	The King and I
Hernando's Hideaway	The Pajama Game
Hey Look Me Over	Wildcat
How to Handle a Woman	Camelot
I Can't Say No	Oklahoma!
I Could be Happy with You	The Boyfriend
I Could Have Danced All Night	My Fair Lady
I Don't Know How to Love Him	Jesus Christ Superstar
I Feel Pretty	West Side Story
I Get a Kick Out of You	Anything Goes
I Got Life	Hair
I Got Plenty O' Nuttin'	Porgy and Bess
I Got Rhythm	Crazy for You
I Hate Men	Kiss Me Kate
I Know Him So Well	Chess
I Talk to the Trees	Paint Your Wagon
I Whistle a Happy Tune	The King and I
I'm Getting Married in the Morning	My Fair Lady
I'm Gonna Wash That Man Right Outta My Hair	South Pacific
I'm Nothing Without You	City of Angels
I've Never Been in Love Before	Guys and Dolls
If Ever I Would Leave You	Camelot
If I Were a Rich Man	Fiddler On the Roof
If My Friends Could See Me Now	Sweet Charity
If the Rains Got to Fall	Half a Sixpence
If You Could talk to the Animals	Doctor Dolittle
It Ain't Necessarily So	Porgy and Bess
It's a Fine Life	Oliver!
Kids	Bye Bye Birdie
Lambeth Walk	Me and My Girl
Leaning On a Lamp Post	Me and My Girl
Let Me Entertain You	Gypsy

TITLE OF SONG	MUSICAL
Love Changes Everything	Aspects of love
Luck be a Lady	Guys and Dolls
Lullaby of Broadway	42nd Street
Make 'Em Laugh	Singin' in the Rain
Memory	Cats
Moses Supposes	Singin' in the Rain
Mr Cellophane	Chicago
Night and Day	Gay Divorce
No Matter What	Whistle Down the Wind
Nobody Does It Like Me	Seesaw
Oh, What a Beautiful Morning	Oklahoma!
Ol' Man River	Show Boat
Once Upon a Dream	Jekyll and Hyde
People	Funny Girl
People Will Say We're in Love	Oklahoma!
Pinball Wizard	Tommy
Put On a Happy Face	Bye Bye Birdie
Rock and Roll is Here to Stay	Grease
Seventy-six Trombones	The Music Man
Sit Down You're Rocking the Boat	Guys and Dolls
Somewhere	West Side Story
Steam Heat	The Pajama Game
Summertime	Porgy and Bess
Take a Letter Miss Jones	Blood Brothers
Take Back Your Mink	Guys and Dolls
Take It On the Chin	Me and My Girl
Tea for Two	No, No, Nanette
Tears On My Pillow	Grease
Thank Heaven For Little Girls	Gigi
Thank You For the Music	Mamma Mia
Thank You Very Much	Scrooge
The Lady is a Tramp	Babes in Arms
The Sun Has Got His Hat On	Me and My Girl
The Time Warp	The Rocky Horror Picture Show
There is Nothing Like a Dame	South Pacific
There's No Business Like Show Business	Annie Get Your Gun
This is the Moment	Jekyll and Hyde
'Til There Was You	The Music Man
Time Heals Everything	Mack and Mabel
Tomorrow	Annie

TITLE OF SONG	MUSICAL
Too Darn Hot	Kiss Me Kate
Tragedy	Saturday Night Fever
True Love	High Society
Two Little Girls From Little Rock	Gentlemen Prefer Blondes
Wandering Star (A)	Paint Your Wagon
We Kiss in a Shadow	The King and I
What I Did For Love	A Chorus Line
What Kind of Fool Am I?	Stop the World – I Want to Get Off
When Children Rule the World	Whistle Down the Wind
Wherever He Ain't	Mack and Mabel
Who Wants to be a Millionaire?	High Society
Wunderbar	Kiss Me Kate
You Are My Lucky Star	Singin' in the Rain
You Can Always Count On Me	City of Angels
You Gotta Get a Gimmick	Gypsy
You're Getting to be a Habit With Me	42nd Street
You're the Top	Anything Goes

Awards

'Pat on the Back Ceremonies' are, for some, just an excuse to get dressed up; for others, they are a good way to get their photo in all the right publications. For the talented élite, it is when they are given the public recognition that 'they got it right!'

There are numerous awards in various categories on both sides of the pond but here we are only interested in the musical categories.

1947 The Tony Awards® were born to celebrate excellence in theatre
1976 Britain follows suit with The Laurence Olivier Awards.

The table below shows which musicals were pronounced the best that year on each side of the pond. Note, the 'Tony' Best Musical category didn't start until 1949)

YEAR	AMERICAN TONY	BRITISH LAURENCE OLIVIER
1949	Kiss Me Kate	
1950	South Pacific	
1951	Guys and Dolls	

YEAR	AMERICAN TONY	BRITISH LAURENCE OLIVIER
1952	The King and I	
1953	Wonderful Town	
1954	Kismet	
1955	The Pajama Game	
1956	Damn Yankees	
1957	My Fair Lady	
1958	The Music Man	
1959	Redhead	
1960	The Sound of Music & Fiorello	
1961	Bye Bye Birdie	
1962	How to Succeed in Business Without Really Trying	
1963	A Funny Thing Happened On the Way to the Forum	
1964	Hello Dolly	
1965	Fiddler On the Roof	
1966	Man of La Mancha	
1967	Cabaret	
1968	Hallelujah Baby	
1969	1776	
1970	Applause	
1971	Company	
1972	Two Gentlemen of Verona	
1973	A Little Night Music	
1974	Raisin	
1975	The Wiz	
1976	A Chorus Line	A Chorus Line
1977	Annie	The Comedy of Errors
1978	Ain't Misbehavin'	Evita
1979	Sweeney Todd	Songbook
1980	Evita	Sweeney Todd
1981	42nd Street	Cats
1982	Nine	Poppy
1983	Cats	Blood Brothers
1984	La Cage aux Folles	42nd Street
1985	Big River	Me and My Girl
1986	The Mystery of Edwin Drood	The Phantom of the Opera
1987	Les Misérables	Follies
1988	The Phantom of the Opera	Candide
1989	Jerome Robbins' Broadway	Return to the Forbidden Planet
1990	City of Angels	Return to the Forbidden Planet

YEAR	AMERICAN TONY	BRITISH LAURENCE OLIVIER
1991	The Will Rogers Follies	Sunday in the Park with George
1992	Crazy for You	Carmen Jones (Revival)
1993	Kiss of the Spider Woman	Crazy for You
1994	Passion	City of Angels
1995	Sunset Boulevard	Once On This Island
1996	Rent	Jolson the Musical
1997	Titanic	Martin Guerre
1998	The Lion King	Beauty and the Beast
1999	Fosse	Kat and The Kings
2000	Contact	Honk! The Ugly Duckling
2001	The Producers	Merrily We Roll Along
2002	Thoroughly Modern Millie	There was no 'Best New Musical Award' this year
2003	Hairspray	Our House
2004	Avenue Q	Jerry Springer the Opera
2005	Monty Python's Spamalot	The Producers
2006	Jersey Boys	Billy Elliot
2007	Spring Awakening	

Chapter Four

Composers and Lyricists of the Twentieth and Twenty-first Centuries

TO WRITE a play, you need a playwright. To write a musical, however, not only do you need a playwright (who in the case of a musical is actually called the librettist), but you also need a composer and a lyricist, and it is these talented individuals who write musicals. These writers fall into one of three categories:

1. **The Classic Writers**
    These writers are often referred to as the 'all time greats'; they laid the modern foundations for today's musical theatre and we are greatly indebted to them. Into this category, fall the likes of Cole Porter, George and Ira Gershwin, Rodgers and Hammerstein and Lerner and Loewe. Many of the younger generation cut their teeth on musicals such as *The King and I* and *My Fair Lady* when they went to their local amateur operatic society's annual performance.

2. **The Established Writers**
    We attribute this term to the likes of Andrew Lloyd Webber, Tim Rice and Boublil and Schönberg, the next generation of writers who had the courage to take musical theatre one step further forward. They introduced us to the 'through-sung' musical using contemporary, sometimes rock, music. At this point, we also saw the theatrical producer grow in strength, becoming more than just a money man – an artist in his own right. Cameron Mackintosh headed this team of new producers with his amazing insight into what the modern audiences wanted alongside the ability to get his writers to deliver just that. However, he is a master of his craft and, unfortunately, not all producers have his gift. Sadly, the result has been that many a musical has failed through a producer trying to emulate Cameron Mackintosh, and

getting it wrong! The tragic thing is that we will never know just how many 'greats' we lost through producer interference.

3. **The New Writers**
   It is now the era of Jason Robert Brown and his contemporaries, who write thought-provoking pieces and complex melodies. And, interestingly, because the world of musical theatre is so well-established and has many years of success upon which it can now draw, we also see more revivals and juke box musicals with their back catalogue of songs. The result being that this is the era of diversity and choice.

There is no doubting the pure genius of these three categories of creators; they are the sole reason why we have flocked to the theatre in our thousands over the decades. So who are they? Well, there are in fact too many to mention, for some creators have written only one or two shows – successful, yes, but continuous, no. There are, however, a few creators who have written many, many hits, or who have shaped music and theatre to such an extent that it is thanks to them that we are, theatrically, in the place in which we find ourselves today. It is these creators whom we will now look at in more detail. However, first we must create one more category, for there are two contributors to musical theatre who are so unique that they just do not sit comfortably into any of the above three, yet they *are* theatre, they *are* musical theatre and they *are* idiosyncratically and quintessentially British. They are a part of the eccentric foundations of our musical theatre culture.

Flamboyant Foundations –
NOEL COWARD V. IVOR NOVELLO

The world of entertainment is noted for its flamboyant and colourful characters and there were none more so than the wonderful Noel Coward and Ivor Novello; they were contemporaries, friends and competitors. Noel Coward once said of Ivor Novello: 'The two loveliest things in the British theatre are Ivor's profile and my mind.'

NOEL COWARD (1899–1973)

When writing about Noel Coward, two words spring to mind, genius and English, for he was, without doubt, a genius as well as being the all-time consummate Englishman. He was a composer, a lyricist, a librettist, a singer, actor, director, painter and novelist, as well as being a man of sophisticated witticism. No wonder he was awarded the nickname 'The Master'.

His achievements were great and numerous. Listed below are Coward's musical productions only:

1916	*The Light Blues*	Actor
1923	*London Calling*	Composer, lyricist, librettist and actor
1925	*On with the Dance*	Composer, lyricist, librettist
1928	*This Year of Grace*	Composer, lyricist, librettist, director and actor
1929	*Bitter Sweet*	Composer, lyricist, librettist and director
1932	*Words and Music*	Composer, lyricist, librettist and director
1934	*Conversation Piece*	Composer, lyricist, librettist, director and actor
1936	*Tonight at 8.30*	Composer, lyricist, librettist, director and actor
1938	*Operette*	Composer, lyricist, librettist, director
1939	*Set to Music*	Composer, lyricist, librettist, and director
1945	*Sigh No More*	Composer, lyricist, librettist and director
1946	*Pacific 1860*	Composer, lyricist, librettist and director
1950	*Ace of Clubs*	Composer, lyricist, librettist and director
1954	*After the Ball*	Composer, lyricist, librettist
1961	*Sail Away*	Composer, lyricist, librettist and director
1963	*The Girl Who Came to Supper*	Composer and lyricist
1964	*High Spirits*	Director

Noel Coward's songs were famous for their wit, probably the most well-known of these being 'Mad Dogs and Englishmen'. The best known of his other songs include:

Dance Little Lady
Dearest Love
Has Anybody Seen Our Ship
I Went to a Marvellous Party
I'll Follow My Secret Heart
I'll See You Again
If Love were All
London Pride
Mad About the Boy

Matelot
Parisian Pierrot
Party's Over Now (The)
Poor Little Rich Girl
Room with a View (A)
Sail Away
Stately Homes of England (The)
Why Do the Wrong People Travel?

And it didn't end there; he also wrote for films and sang in nightclubs; he wrote 25 non-musical plays and recorded his own compositions.

IVOR NOVELLO (1893–1951)

Ivor Novello, composer, singer and actor was as well-known for his outstanding beauty as he was for his outstanding talent. During his lifetime he wrote 22 plays and seven extremely popular British operettas, six of these with Christopher Hassall as lyricist; extraordinarily, and bearing in mind the fact that he couldn't sing, he also appeared in six himself, but he left the actual singing to others in his cast.

1916	*Theodore and Co*	Composer
1917	*Arlette*	Composer
1918	*Tabs*	Composer
1919	*Who's Hooper?*	Composer
1921	*The Golden Moth*	Composer
1924	*Puppets*	Composer
1929	*The House That Jack Built*	Composer
1935	*Glamorous Night*	Composer
1936	*Careless Rapture*	Composer
1937	*Crest of the Wave*	Composer
1939	*The Dancing Years*	Composer
1943	*Arc de Triomphe*	Composer
1945	*Perchance to Dream*	Composer
1949	*King's Rhapsody*	Composer
1951	*Gay's the Word*	Composer

In addition to his stage successes, Ivor was responsible for the international, First World War hit song, 'Keep the Home Fires Burning'. He also spent some time in Hollywood as an actor where he appeared in several silent films, but his first love was always the stage.

Just months after *Gay's the Word* opened to rave revues, Ivor Novello returned home to his flat above the – now named in his honour – Novello Theatre in London, where he died of a coronary thrombosis. His funeral was as flamboyant as his life and was broadcast on national radio. Thousands lined the streets, women outnumbering men, despite his being homosexual. They were probably attracted to his sentimental nature and love of romance, plus the fact that he was reputedly a warm-hearted and even-tempered man.

As well as having a theatre named after him, Ivor Novello also has an award ceremony named after him, affectionately known as the Ivors.

Noel Coward and Ivor Novello were quintessentially eccentric and flamboyant British gentlemen who epitomised talent and theatre in equal doses. One does wonder whether we will ever see such splendid theatrical eccentricity again. If we do, I doubt that we will ever be fortunate enough to encounter two such geniuses born at the same time again.

Lionel Bart

WELL-KNOWN SHOWS

Fings Ain't Wot They Used T'Be (1959) • *Oliver!* (1960) • *Blitz!* (1962) • *Maggie May* (1964)

WELL-KNOWN SONGS

Fings Ain't Wot They used T'Be (*Fings Ain't Wot They used T'Be*) • Food, Glorious Food; Consider Yourself; As Long as He Needs Me (*Oliver!*)

THE MAJOR MILESTONES ON LIONEL BART'S MUSICAL JOURNEY

1930	Lionel Bart is born Lionel Begleiter on 1 August, the youngest child of a large, East End, Jewish family. He later changes his surname to Bart, after St. Barts, the London hospital.
1936	His parents give him an old violin after being told by a teacher that he is a musical genius, but they soon stop his lessons when he doesn't work; in fact, he never did learn to read music and, later on in life, had to sing his compositions into a tape recorder.

1946	Lionel is given a scholarship to St Martin's School of Art, but is expelled.
1956	He discovers Tommy Hicks performing guitar in a Soho coffee bar; Tommy Hicks is later to become Tommy Steele.
1960	*Oliver!* opens at the New Theatre (Albery Theatre), London, on 30 June where it was given a staggering 23 curtain calls.
1960	Lionel is given the Variety Club Silver Heart for Show Business Personality of the Year.
1962	*Blitz!* with music and lyrics solely by Lionel Bart and book by Lionel Bart and Joan Maitland, opens at the Adelphi Theatre, London.
1963	*Oliver!* opens on Broadway.
1964	*Maggie May*, again with music and lyrics by Lionel and book by Alun Owen, opens at the Adelphi Theatre London.
1965	Lionel's musical *Twang!!* opens, only to flop.

Then followed the dark years
which spanned 20 years

- Lionel makes a huge mistake and descends into his 'Dark Years' when he tries to salvage *Twang!!* with his own money.
- He sells the rights to his past and future works, including *Oliver!* in an attempt to keep himself solvent.

1972	He declares himself bankrupt and spends the next decade drinking heavily.
1975	Lionel is banned from driving for being under the influence of drink.
1983	He is banned from driving again, this time for two years. He joins Alcoholics Anonymous and re-takes control of his life.

Lionel Bart
Born: 1 August 1930
Died: 3 April 1999

1986	Lionel receives a special Ivor Novello Award for his life's achievement.
1994	Lionel partly rewrites *Oliver!* and Cameron Mackintosh, who owns half the rights, revives the musical at the London Palladium, magnanimously giving Lionel a share of the production royalties.
1999	3 April, Lionel Bart dies in London of cancer, aged 68.

OVERVIEW

Lionel first gained widespread recognition through his songwriting; it was he who wrote the immortal hit, 'Living Doll', for Cliff Richard, and the hits for Tommy Steele – 'Handful of Songs', 'Butterfingers' and 'Little White Bull'. He won several Ivor Novello Awards for his songwriting.

The story of Lionel Bart epitomises the sadness and despair that genius and success can bring if it catches us with our guard down, but it also shows us the other side of the coin in the guise of Cameron Mackintosh, and the generosity and compassion he showed towards Lionel Bart.

Irving Berlin

WELL-KNOWN SHOWS

Annie Get Your Gun (1946) • *Call Me Madam* (1950)

WELL-KNOWN SONGS

There's No Business Like Show Business; Doin' What Comes Natur'lly; You Can't Get a Man With a Gun (*Annie Get Your Gun*) • It's a Lovely Day Today (*Call Me Madam*)

THE MAJOR MILESTONES ON IRVING BERLIN'S MUSICAL JOURNEY

1888	Irving Berlin is born Israel Baline on 11 May in Siberia, Russia, the son of Jewish cantor Isadore Baline and the youngest of eight children.
1893	Israel moves with his family to America.
1896	His father dies and eight-year-old Israel is forced to work to survive.

1906	Israel is hired as a singing waiter at Pelham's. It is while here that he is asked to write the lyrics for a song. When published, a printer's error on the front cover gave Israel Baline the name Irving Berlin and that's the way it stayed.
1911	Irving has his first major international hit – *Alexander's Ragtime Band.*
1912	Irving Berlin marries Dorothy Goetz but, tragically, she contracts typhoid when they are on honeymoon and dies soon after their return home. The death of his wife inspired some of his most heart-rending compositions, one being 'When I Lost You'.
1918	During the First World War, Irving joins the army and writes songs to help national morale. He also writes a stage piece, entitled *Yip Yip Yaphank*, to be performed only by soldiers.
1921	Together with Sam Harris, Irving builds the Music Box Theatre as a venue for his own music and for other shows.
1926	Irving marries Ellin Mackay.
1932	After a few musically barren years, Irving writes the stage show *Face the Music.*
1933	He sees his stage show *As Thousands Cheer* open on Broadway, which features a song that is to become one of his most famous, 'Easter Parade'.

In the 1930s, films were a great part of the entertainment industry and Irving embraced this culture as a way to expose his music to a more extensive audience.

1937	A song originally written for *Yip Yip Yaphank*, but never used, is reworked to become the great patriotic song 'God Bless America' for which Irving wins many awards and earns huge royalties.
1940	*This is the Army* premières on Broadway. Irving donated all the royalties from this show to charity – which amounted to several million dollars.
1946	*Annie Get Your Gun* opens on Broadway for which Irving wrote both the music and lyrics, while Herbert and Dorothy Fields wrote the book.

1950	*Call Me Madam* opens on Broadway, with music and lyrics by Irving and book by Howard Lindsay and Russell Crouse.
1952	*Call Me Madam* opens in the West End.
1960s	After the 1960s, Berlin retired from active composing.
1989	Irving Berlin dies on 22 September in New York.

OVERVIEW

After Irving Berlin retired, it became clear that he had left us with a musical legacy of unrivalled melodies and lyrics from songs such as: 'Alexander's Ragtime Band'; 'A Pretty Girl Is Like A Melody'; 'Easter Parade'; 'How Deep is The Ocean'; 'White Christmas'; 'God Bless America' and 'There's No Business Like Show Business'. He also composed the scores for 19 film musicals including: *Top Hat* (1935) and *White Christmas* (1954). Irving could never be truly described as a musician for he did not actually play an instrument and could only just play the piano – and then only in the key of F! He employed arrangers to write down his melodies for him and some people – unnecessarily – speculate that perhaps he employed not arrangers but ghost-writers. Some think that it is not possible to write such wonderful melodies unless you are a musician. I wholeheartedly disagree. I have seen at first hand a young 'composer' give an arranger the basic melody and then go on to instruct, in detail, the full arrangement for the song. This young composer is, as Irving Berlin was, unable to transfer what is in the head to the hands and, like Irving Berlin, has been hailed as a genius. Irving Berlin wrote music to shape music; the method he used was totally irrelevant.

Don Black

WELL-KNOWN SHOWS

Tell Me On a Sunday (1979) • *Aspects of Love* (1989)• *Sunset Boulevard* (1993)

WELL-KNOWN SONGS

In One of My Weaker Moments (*Budgie*) • Take That Look Off Your Face; Tell Me On a Sunday (*Tell Me On a Sunday*)

THE MAJOR MILESTONES ON DON BLACK'S MUSICAL JOURNEY

1938 Don Black is born on 21 June 1938; he spends his early working life as an office boy before moving on to become a song plugger; he also works as a stand-up comedian.

1966 *Born Free* is released, for which he collaborated with John Barry to write the title song.

1974 *Billy* the musical opens in the West End, with lyrics by Don Black and music by John Barry.

1978 *Bar Mitzvah Boy* opens in the West End, for which Don wrote the lyrics to Jule Styne's music

1979 *Tell Me On a Sunday*, for which Don wrote the lyrics to Andrew Lloyd Webber's music, plays at Andrew Lloyd Webber's Sydmonton Festival.

1980 *Tell Me On a Sunday* opens in the West End.

1980 *Tell Me On a Sunday* is broadcast on television.

1988 *Budgie* the musical, for which Don wrote the lyrics, opens in the West End.

1989 *Aspects of Love* opens in the West End, with lyrics by Don Black (and Charles Hart).

1990 *Aspects of Love* opens on Broadway.

1992 *Starlight Express* is revamped with additional lyrics by Don Black.

1993 *Sunset Boulevard* opens in the West End with lyrics by Don Black and Christopher Hampton.

1993 *Sunset Boulevard* opens in Los Angeles.

1994 *Sunset Boulevard* opens on Broadway.

2003 A revised version of *Tell Me On a Sunday* opens in the West End with additional material by Jackie Clune.

2004 *Dracula* opens on Broadway with lyrics once more by Don Black and Christopher Hampton; the music is by Frank Wildhorn.

2007 *Dracula* opens in Switzerland.

2007 He is inducted into the Songwriters Hall of Fame.

OVERVIEW

Lyricists are surely as important as composers? Without them there would just be a tune. All musicals need a lyricist and Don Black is prolific in the extreme. In addition to writing lyrics for stage musicals, Don has written over 100 songs for films; he has had hit songs on both sides of the Atlantic and has worked with some of the world's leading composers, including Andrew Lloyd Webber and Marvin Hamlisch.

Alain Boublil and Claude-Michel Schönberg

WELL-KNOWN SHOWS

Les Misérables (1985) • *Miss Saigon* (1989) • *Martin Guerre* (1996)

WELL-KNOWN SONGS

I Dreamed a Dream; On My Own; Bring Him Home (*Les Misérables*) • The Last Night of the World; I'd Give My Life for You; Why God Why (*Miss Saigon*)

THE MAJOR MILESTONES ON ALAIN BOUBLIL'S MUSICAL JOURNEY

1941   Alain is born in Tunisia.

1959   Alain moves to Paris, France where he works in music publishing before beginning his famous collaborations with Claude-Michel Schönberg.

1973   *La Révolution Française* opens in Paris, the first ever rock-opera/musical to be written in France. Alain invites Claude-Michel Schönberg to be part of the team of four writers.

1980   *Les Misérables* – for which he wrote the book (along with Claude-Michel Schönberg) and lyrics while Claude-Michel Schönberg also wrote the music – opens at the Palais des Sports, Paris.

1983   Alain collaborates with ABBA (Benny Andersson and Björn Ulvaeus) and co-lyricist Daniel Boublil, on a children's musical, *Abbacadabra*, using the music of ABBA.

1984   It is Christmas and *Abbacadabra* plays in London at the Lyric, Hammersmith.

1985   In October, *Les Misérables* opens at the Barbican, London, moving to the Palace Theatre in December of the same year.

1987   *Les Misérables* opens on Broadway.

Alain Boublil
Born: 5 March 1941

Claude-Michel Schönberg
Born: 6 July 1944

1989 *Miss Saigon* opens in London, with book and lyrics by Alain and book and music by his writing partner Claude-Michel Schönberg; it goes on to be another massive hit for the French pair.

1996 *Martin Guerre,* another Boublil/Schönberg collaboration, opens in London, but it never achieves the success of *Les Misérables* and *Miss Saigon.*

2003 *Les Demoiselles de Rochefort,* Alain's stage adaptation, in collaboration with Michel Legrand, of Jacques Demy's film, plays in Paris.

2007 Alain Boublil's latest musical *The Pirate Queen* opens in Chicago and then on Broadway, with music once more by Claude-Michel Schönberg, but it is generally not well received, closing after 180 performances.

2007 *Martin Guerre* opens at The Watermill in Newbury.

2008 *Marguerite* the musical with the book by Alain Boublil and Claude-Michel Schönberg, lyrics by Herbert Kretzmer and music by Michel Legrand opens at the Haymarket, London.

THE MAJOR MILESTONES ON CLAUDE-MICHEL SCHÖNBERG'S MUSICAL JOURNEY

1944	Claude-Michel is born in Vannes, France of Hungarian parents.
1970s	He becomes a successful record producer and singer.
1973	*La Révolution Française* opens in Paris.
1980	*Les Misérables* with music by Claude-Michel, and lyrics by his writing partner Alain Boublil, opens at the Palais des Sports, Paris.
1985	In October, *Les Misérables*, opens at the Barbican, London, moving to the Palace Theatre in December of the same year.
1987	*Les Misérables* opens on Broadway
1989	*Miss Saigon* opens in London; another Boublil/Schönberg musical, which goes on to be a massive hit for the French pair.
1996	*Martin Guerre* opens in London but never achieves the success of *Les Misérables* and *Miss Saigon*.
2001	Claude-Michel composes his first ballet score, *Wuthering Heights*.
2003	He marries English ballerina, Charlotte Talbot.
2007	Boublil and Schönberg's latest musical, *The Pirate Queen* opens in Chicago and then on Broadway, but is generally not well received, closing after 180 performances.

OVERVIEW

Alain has also written plays for the stage and, in 2003, had his first novel published, *Les Dessous de Soi*, winning the French Prince Maurice Award for romantic fiction. But it is as a writing team in the world of musical theatre that Alain Boublil and Claude-Michel Schönberg are best known and where they have become one of the more well-known musical theatre collaboration teams to emerge in the last 20 years – and more amazingly, out of France, a country famed for its amazing cuisine but not for its contribution to the world of musical theatre. Although the driving force behind their musicals, they do always work with other creators; this is a language decision. Alain writes all their shows in French first and then decides on an English adaptator. Two names frequently appear. They are Herbert Kretzmer and Richard Maltby Jr.

HERBERT KRETZMER
Born: 1925, Kroonstad, S. Africa
- Herbert enjoyed an outstanding journalistic career.
- He has also enjoyed an outstanding career as a lyricist of both pop songs and songs for musical theatre.

RICHARD MALTBY JR
Born: 6 October 1937, Wisconsin, America
- Richard is also a renowned stage director.
- In addition to writing lyrics, he also writes screenplays.
- It is said that he also devises crossword puzzles.

Jason Robert Brown

WELL-KNOWN SHOWS

Songs for a New World (1995) • *The Last Five Years* (2001) • *Parade* (1998)• *13* (2007)

WELL-KNOWN SONGS

The New World; Christmas Lullaby; Stars and the Moon (*Songs for a New World*) • The Old Red Hills of Home; All the Wasted Time (*Parade*) • Still Hurting; Shiksa Goddess; The Next Ten Minutes; Goodbye Until Tomorrow (*The Last Five Years*) • Mr Hopalong Heartbreak (*Urban Cowboy*) • What It Means to be a Friend (*13*)

Jason Robert Brown
Born: 20 June 1970

THE MAJOR MILESTONES ON JASON ROBERT BROWN'S MUSICAL JOURNEY

1970 Jason is born in Tarrytown, New York, the second son of Deborah, an English teacher, and Stuart Brown, a salesman.

1977 At the age of seven he begins piano lessons; he writes his first song at the age of 10 and goes on to première his first full-length musical comedy at his summer camp in 1986, when he is just 16 years old.

1987 Jason studies composition at the Eastman School of Music in Rochester, New York under Samuel Adler and Joseph Schwantner. He leaves after two years to teach at a performing arts high school in Miami.

1990 He moves to New York City to become a musical director and writer; he plays for many cabaret artists, including the Tonics (with whom he makes his Carnegie Hall debut at a 1992 tribute for Stephen Sondheim).

1994 He conducts and arranges the premières of off-Broadway musicals by Yoko Ono and Michael John LaChiusa.

1995 *Songs for a New World* – musical revue premières off Broadway for which he wrote the music and lyrics and in which he both conducts and plays the piano; it is a piece conceived and directed by Daisy Prince, daughter of Hal Prince.

1998 Jason's musical *Parade* co-written with Alfred Uhry, for which he wrote both the music and lyrics, premières at the Lincoln Center; the piece was commissioned by Hal Prince.

2000 Jason conducts the American National tour of *Parade*.

2001 *The Last Five Years*, book, music and lyrics by Jason premières in Skokie, Illinois.

2001 *Songs for a New World* opens at the Bridewell Theatre in London.

2002 *The Last Five Years* opens in New York. Jason conducts and contributes five songs to *Urban Cowboy: The Musical* on Broadway. He also sings the second act opening number.

2003 Jason marries composer Georgia Stitt with whom he has a daughter.

2006 *The Last Five Years* opens at the Menier Chocolate Factory in London.

2007 Jason's new musical, *13*, which he co-wrote with Dan Elish, premières in Los Angeles.

2007 *Parade* makes its UK debut at the Donmar Warehouse, London.

2008 *13* opens on Broadway.

OVERVIEW

Jason Robert Brown is one of this century's 'New Writers'; his thought-provoking and ground-breaking approach to musical theatre is loved and admired by the new generation of young theatre goers. For a musician, as well as for a singer, his compositions with their rhythmically challenging structure are not an easy ride and require an intelligent and thoughtful approach. For this reason, students of musical theatre frequently feel a surge of satisfaction when they 'nail their performance' of a Jason Robert Brown song. Unlike many composers, Jason frequently performs his own work, sometimes with his own band and sometimes without. He also teaches Musical Theatre Performance at the University of Southern California.

Cy Coleman

WELL-KNOWN SHOWS

Sweet Charity (1966) • *Barnum* (1980) • *City of Angels* (1989)

WELL-KNOWN SONGS

Big Spender; If My Friends Could See Me Now (*Sweet Charity*) • The Colours of My Life (*Barnum*) • You Can Always Count On Me (*City of Angels*)

THE MAJOR MILESTONES ON CY COLEMAN'S MUSICAL JOURNEY

1929 Cy is born Seymour Kaufman on 14 June in New York to Eastern European Jewish parents; he is brought up in the Bronx.

1936 A child prodigy (piano), he makes his debut at Carnegie Hall.

1960 *Wildcat* opens on Broadway featuring the well-known song 'Hey Look Me Over'; lyrics by Carolyn Leigh and book by N. Richard Nash.

1962 *Little Me*, a musical comedy, opens on Broadway with lyrics once more by Carolyn Leigh and the book by Neil Simon; the great Bob Fosse is co-director and he also stages the musical numbers and dances.

1964 *Little Me* opens in the West End

1964 Coleman meets his future writing partner, Dorothy Fields.

1966 *Sweet Charity* opens on Broadway with Dorothy Fields having written the lyrics and Neil Simon the book.

1967 *Sweet Charity* opens in the West End.

1973 *Seesaw* opens on Broadway, again with Dorothy Fields writing the lyrics; the book, this time, is by Michael Stewart.

1974 Dorothy Fields dies, bringing a great partnership to an untimely end.

1977 *I Love My Wife* opens on Broadway, the result of a collaboration between Cy and Michael Stewart who wrote the book and lyrics.

1977 *I Love My Wife* opens in the West End.

1978 *On the Twentieth Century* opens on Broadway with the book and lyrics by Betty Comden and Adolph Green.

1980 *On the Twentieth Century* opens in the West End.

1980 *Barnum* opens on Broadway with lyrics by Michael Stewart and book by Mark Bramble.

1981 *Barnum* opens in the West End

1989 *City of Angels* opens on Broadway, with lyrics by David Zippel and book by Larry Gelbart.

1991 *Will Rogers Follies* opens on Broadway, with lyrics by Betty Comden, Adolph Green and book by Peter Stone, inspired by the words of Will and Betty Rogers.

1997 *The Life* opens on Broadway, with lyrics by Ira Gasman and book by David Newman, Ira Gasman and Cy Coleman.

2004 Cy Coleman dies on 18 November of a heart attack in New York at the age of 75 years.

OVERVIEW

Cy Coleman began his life as a classically trained pianist – a child prodigy. He moved from classical music to jazz and then on to popular music; working with a variety of lyricists he remained involved in theatre right up until his death, passing away just after he had attended the première of Michael Frayn's new play *Democracy*.

Noel Coward (see page 101)

Fred Ebb (see page 123)

Dorothy Fields

WELL-KNOWN SHOWS

Annie Get Your Gun (1946) • *Sweet Charity* (1966) • *Seesaw* (1973)

WELL-KNOWN SONGS

Big Spender; If My Friends Could See Me Now; The Rhythm of Life (*Sweet Charity*) • It's Not Where You Start; Nobody Does It Like Me (*Seesaw*) •

The Way You Look Tonight; Pick Yourself Up; A Fine Romance (from the film *Swing Time*)

THE MAJOR MILESTONES ON DOROTHY FIELDS' MUSICAL JOURNEY

1905   Dorothy is born on 15 July in New Jersey into a theatrical family; the youngest child of actor Lew Fields and his wife Rose, she had an older sister and two older brothers, including Herbert. Her brothers were both later to become successful playwrights. Upon leaving school, Dorothy begins work as a Drama teacher.

1924   She marries Dr Jack Wiener.

1928   A song Dorothy had written earlier – 'I Can't Give You Anything But Love' – is used in the show *Blackbirds* and goes on to be a huge success.

1930s   Now based in Hollywood, Dorothy writes many of her wonderful songs for films, including songs for *Swing Time* starring Fred Astaire and Ginger Rogers – on this film, her collaborator was Jerome Kern.

1939   Having divorced her first husband, Dorothy marries Eli Lahm, with whom she goes on to have two children. They move to New York.

1946   *Annie Get Your Gun* opens on Broadway, for which Dorothy co-wrote the book with her brother Herbert Fields; Irving Berlin wrote the music and lyrics.

1953   *A Tree Grows in Brooklyn*.

1966   *Sweet Charity* opens on Broadway, the result of collaboration with Cy Coleman who wrote the music and Neil Simon who wrote the book.

1967   *Sweet Charity* opens in the West End.

1973   *Seesaw* opens on Broadway, with lyrics by Dorothy, music by Cy Coleman and book by Michael Stewart.

1974   Dorothy dies on 28 March in New York.

OVERVIEW

Dorothy Fields is one of the least celebrated lyricists of the last century and yet one of the greatest, and certainly one of the most diverse and forward thinking. Unlike many lyricists, she worked with a variety of composers in her lifetime – Irving Berlin, Jerome Kern and Cy Coleman being just three. Dorothy's work travelled in every artistic direction, from one-off songs through the world of films and into musicals. In her life-time, Dorothy wrote the lyrics for 10 musicals and 12 musical revues; she also wrote the book for eight musicals and, in addition, wrote over 400 songs – another example of the fact that it's not just the music that makes a great song.

George and Ira Gershwin

George Gershwin
Born: 26 September 1898
Died: 11 June 1937

Ira Gershwin
Born: 6 December 1896
Died: 17 August 1983

WELL-KNOWN SHOWS

Lady be Good (1923) • *Funny Face* (1927) • *Crazy for You* (1992) • *Porgy and Bess* (1935)

WELL-KNOWN SONGS

Someone to Watch Over Me; Embraceable You; I Got Rhythm; Nice Work If You Can Get It (*Crazy for You*) • Fascinating Rhythm (*Lady be Good*) • Summertime; I Got Plenty o' Nuttin'; It Ain't Necessarily So (*Porgy and Bess*) • S'Wonderful (*Funny Face*)

THE MAJOR MILESTONES ON GEORGE GERSHWIN'S MUSICAL JOURNEY

1898   Jacob (George) Gershovitz is born in Brooklyn, New York. The son of Russian-Jewish immigrant parents, he has two brothers, Arthur and Ira – who became his writing partner – and a sister, Frances (Frankie). George learns to play the piano, on a piano which was originally bought for his brother Ira.

1919   *Swanee* with music by George and lyrics by Irving Caesar premières at the Capital Revue and goes on to become a massive hit when Al Jolson sings it.

1924   Première of *Rhapsody in Blue.*

1924   *Lady be Good*, which George has written with his brother Ira, opens on Broadway.

1926   *Lady be Good* opens in the West End

1927   *Funny Face*, again written with Ira, opens on Broadway.

1928   *Funny Face* opens in the West End.

1930   *Girl Crazy*, with lyrics by Ira, opens on Broadway.

1931   *Of Thee I Sing*, again with music by George and lyrics by Ira, opens at the Music Box Theatre on Broadway, book by George S. Kaufman and Morrie Ryskind; this was the first Pulitzer Prize-winning musical.

1935   *Porgy and Bess*, another Gershwin brothers' collaboration, opens at the Alvin Theatre in New York, with music by George, and lyrics by Ira and DuBose Heyward. Sadly, it was a flop for the brothers at the time.

1937   George dies in Los Angeles of a brain tumour at a tragically premature age.

1942   A successful revival of *Porgy and Bess* is mounted too late for George to enjoy.

1992   *Crazy for You* (a revised version of *Girl Crazy*) opens on Broadway, long after both George and Ira's death.

1993   *Crazy for You* opens in the West End.

THE MAJOR MILESTONES ON IRA GERSHWIN'S MUSICAL JOURNEY

1896   Israel (Ira) Gershovitz is born in New York City. The son of Russian-Jewish immigrant parents, he has two brothers, Arthur and George – who became his writing partner – and a sister, Frances (Frankie).

1919   Ira has his first Broadway hit with *Two Little Girls in Blue*, with music by Vincent Youmans and Paul Lanin, book by Fred Jackson.

1924	*Lady be Good*, which Ira has written with his brother George, opens on Broadway.
1924	Ira marries Leonore Strunsky.
1926	*Lady be Good*, opens in the West End.
1927	*Funny Face*, again written with George, opens on Broadway.
1928	*Funny Face* opens in the West End.
1930	*Girl Crazy*, with music by George, opens on Broadway.
1931	*Of Thee I Sing*, again with music by George and lyrics by Ira, opens at the Music Box Theatre on Broadway, book by George S. Kaufman and Morrie Ryskind; this was the first Pulitzer Prize-winning musical.
1935	*Porgy and Bess*, another Gershwin brothers' collaboration, opens at the Alvin Theatre in New York with music by George, and lyrics by DuBose Heyward and Ira Gershwin. Sadly, it was a flop for the brothers at the time.
1937	George dies of a brain tumour at a tragically premature age.
1941	*Lady in the Dark* opens at the Alvin Theatre with music by Kurt Weil and book by Moss Hart.
1942	A successful revival of *Porgy and Bess* is mounted, but it is too late for Ira to share the joy of success with his late brother, George.
1983	Ira dies peacefully at his Beverly Hills home, 46 years after his brother George.
1992	*Crazy for You* (a revised version of *Girl Crazy*) opens on Broadway, long after both George and Ira's death.
1993	*Crazy for You* opens in the West End.

OVERVIEW

What a great song book these brothers left to the world – many people actually believe them to be a husband and wife writing team. In June 1983, the name of the renowned Uris Theatre on Broadway was officially changed to the Gershwin Theatre in honour of the two brothers, who as well as contributing many musicals to the Uris, had also seen their opera *Porgy and Bess* open there. It was a great honour that at least Ira lived long enough to see.

Oscar Hammerstein II (see page 131)

Lorenz Hart (see page 131)

Sir Elton John

WELL-KNOWN SHOWS

The Lion King (1997) • *Aida* (1998) • *Billy Elliot* (2005) • *Lestat* (2006)

WELL-KNOWN SONGS

Every Story is a Love Story; Written in the Stars (*Aida*) • Circle of Life; I Just Can't Wait to be King; Hakuna Matata; Can You Feel the Love Tonight (*The Lion King*) • Electricity (*Billy Elliot*)

Sir Elton John
Born: 25 March 1947

THE MAJOR MILESTONES ON ELTON JOHN'S MUSICAL JOURNEY

1947 Born Reginald Kenneth Dwight in Pinner, England, the son of Stanley and Sheila; he later changes his name to Elton John.

1951 Little Elton John begins to play the piano.

1959 He begins his studies at the Royal Academy of Music in London.

1961 Elton joins his first group, Bluesology.

1967 Ray Williams of Liberty Records introduces Elton to Bernie Taupin. This is the start of the famous Elton John/Bernie Taupin songwriting team.

1968 Elton and Bernie become staff songwriters for Dick James' DJM label, writing songs for up and coming pop stars, including Lulu.

1969 Elton releases his debut album, *Empty Sky*, for DJM.

1970s Throughout this and the next three decades, Elton continues to write and perform pop music, achieving many international best-selling singles and albums.

1976 A long-time supporter of Watford Football Club, he becomes its Chairman.

1984 Elton marries Renate Blauel; this marriage is dissolved in 1988.

1990 He is made President of Watford Football Club.

1992 He establishes the Elton John Aids Foundation.

1990s While this decade sees his advent into the world of musical theatre, it also heralds a heartbreaking period for him with the loss of two close friends, Diana, Princess of Wales and fashion design guru, Gianni Versace.

1994 He is inducted into the Rock 'n Roll Hall of Fame.

1994 Elton collaborates with lyricist Tim Rice on songs for Disney's animated feature film *The Lion King*.

1997 The stage version of the musical *The Lion King* premières at The Orpheum Theatre before moving onto Broadway. The book is by Roger Allers and Irene Mecchi; additional music and lyrics are by Lebo M., Mark Mancini, Jay Rifkin and Julie Taymore.

1997 Elton performs 'Candle in the Wind 1997', a rewrite of his Marilyn Monroe tribute, at Diana's funeral and it later becomes the biggest selling single ever in the world – and to date still is, with little chance of that changing.

1998 Elton is knighted Sir Elton Hercules John by Queen Elizabeth II for 'services to music and charitable services'.

1999 *The Lion King* opens in the West End.

2000 *Aida* opens on Broadway, with music by Elton John, lyrics by Tim Rice and a book by Linda Woolverton, Robert Falls and David Henry Hwang.

2002 He is awarded an honorary doctorate from the Royal Academy of Music.

2004 *The Red Piano* show opens at the Caesars Palace Colosseum in Las Vegas, with Elton at the helm.

2005 *Billy Elliot* opens in the West End with music by Elton John and book and lyrics by Lee Hall.

2005 Elton is joined in a civil partnership with his long-term partner, David Furnish.

2005 Elton and Bernie begin to work on the musical *Lestat*.

2006 *Lestat* opens on Broadway with the music by Elton, the lyrics by Bernie Taupin and the book by Linda Woolverton.

OVERVIEW

As well as writing for musical theatre, Elton John's parallel pop career as a singer/songwriter has spanned more than 35 years. He is one of the most flamboyant and outrageous artists of modern times and it is these very qualities which endear him to the public. His generosity is legendary and his talent limitless, and long may it continue that way.

John Kander and Fred Ebb

WELL-KNOWN SHOWS

Cabaret (1966) • *Chicago* (1975) • *Kiss of the Spider Woman* (1993) •

WELL-KNOWN SONGS

Cabaret; Don't Tell Mamma (*Cabaret*) • All That Jazz; When You're Good to Mamma; Mr Cellophane; Razzle Dazzle (*Chicago*)

THE MAJOR MILESTONES ON JOHN KANDER'S MUSICAL JOURNEY

1927	John Kander is born on 18 March in Kansas City, Missouri.
1933	John begins piano lessons and goes on to study music at the Conservatory of Music in Kansas.
1955	He is made Choral Director and Conductor for the Warwick Musical Theatre in Rhode Island; a post he holds until 1958.
1962	John makes his Broadway debut with *A Family Affair*, book by James and William Goldman and lyrics by James Goldman and Jolin Kander; sadly, it is not a success.

THE MAJOR MILESTONES ON FRED EBB'S MUSICAL JOURNEY

1932	Fred Ebb is born on 8 April in New York City.
1952	Aged only 20, he is already writing songs and, more importantly, getting paid for doing so.
1953	Together with the composer Phil Springer, Fred is hired by Columbia to write a song for Judy Garland; it is his first published song.

THE MAJOR MILESTONES ON KANDER AND EBB'S MUSICAL JOURNEY AS THEY TRAVEL TOGETHER

1963	John and Fred are introduced to each other by their mutual publisher.
1965	*Flora the Red Menace*, music and lyrics by John and Fred, book by George Abbott and Robert Russell, opens on

Broadway; it is in this musical that Liza Minnelli makes her Broadway debut.

1966   *Cabaret*, with music and lyrics by the pair and book by Joe Masteroff, opens on Broadway; this musical is destined to be their greatest work.

1975   *Chicago*, music by John Kander and lyrics by Fred Ebb (Fred also wrote the book with Bob Fosse), opens on Broadway. It is not, however, the success it is later to become.

1977   *The Act* opens on Broadway with music and lyrics by John and Fred; book by George Furth.

1977   Kander and Ebb write their most famous song: 'New York, New York', which Frank Sinatra made into a massive hit for the pair. Together, they continue to write.

1978   *Zorba*, with book by Joseph Stein, opens on Broadway.

1981   *Woman of the Year*, with book by Peter Stone, opens on Broadway.

1984   *The Rink*, with book by Terence McNally, opens on Broadway.

1988   *The Rink* opens in the West End.

1992   *Kiss of the Spider Woman*, with book by Terence McNally, opens in the West End.

1993   *Kiss of the Spider Woman* opens on Broadway.

1997   A revival of *Chicago* proves to be the massive hit it failed to be the first time around.

1998   John Kander and Fred Ebb are honoured with Lifetime Achievement awards at the 21st Kennedy Center Honors.

2002   The film version of *Chicago* becomes the first musical in over 30 years to win an Academy Award for Best Picture.

2004   A writing collaboration spanning four decades is brought to a sad end with Fred Ebb's death on 11 September.

2007   The murder mystery musical, *Curtains*, which the pair were working on when Fred died, opens on Broadway with the book by Peter Stone and additional lyrics by John Kander and Rupert Holmes.

OVERVIEW

The writing collaboration of John Kander and Fred Ebb lasted longer than many marriages and only ended with Fred Ebb's death in 2004, but he left behind a rich legacy. Together, the pair wrote for films as well as stage musicals and for singers such as Barbra Streisand, Lauren Bacall, Frank

Sinatra and Chita Rivera. The singer, however, most closely associated with their style is Liza Minnelli, who is well-known for her powerful renditions of 'Cabaret' and 'New York, New York'.

Herbert Kretzmer (see page 113)

Alan Jay Lerner and Frederick Loewe

WELL-KNOWN SHOWS

Brigadoon (1947) • *Paint Your Wagon* (1951) • *My Fair Lady* (1956) • *Camelot* (1960) • *Gigi* (1973)

WELL-KNOWN SONGS

Almost Like Being in Love; The Heather On the Hill (*Brigadoon*) • Thank Heaven for Little Girls; The Night They Invented Champagne (*Gigi*) • Wand'rin' Star; I Talk to the Trees (*Paint Your Wagon*) • Wouldn't It Be Loverly; With a Little Bit of Luck; I Could Have Danced All Night; On The Street Where You Live; Get Me to the Church On Time (*My Fair Lady*) • How to Handle a Woman; If Ever I Would Leave You (*Camelot*)

THE MAJOR MILESTONES ON FREDERICK LOEWE'S MUSICAL JOURNEY

1904	Frederick (Fritz) Loewe is born on 10 June in Vienna, Austria. The son of an opera singer, Edmund and his wife Rosa, he is educated in Berlin where he also grows up.
1911	By the age of seven, Fritz can pick up scores by ear, which means that he can help his father rehearse; he is fast becoming a fine musician.
1923	He is awarded the Höllander Medal in Berlin and goes on to study composition and orchestration.
1925	The Loewe family move to America.
1930s	In America, Frederick begins composing for the theatre, but with little success and, as a result, he lives in near poverty.
1942	Fritz accidentally bumps into Alan Jay Lerner at the Lamb's Club in New York City, thus heralding the start of their successful partnership. Together, they write *Great Lady*, not a huge success but a start, and from there they go on to

write *The Day Before Spring*, again not a huge success but better; the pair are on the verge of something big.

1947 Success comes in the form of *Brigadoon*; this is then followed by more hits.

1951 *Paint Your Wagon* opens on Broadway.

1956 *My Fair Lady* opens on Broadway and is set to become the longest running musical of all time, until the record is broken by Andrew Lloyd Webber's *Cats*.

1958 *Gigi* – the film version of this musical – wins nine Academy Awards.

1960 *Camelot* opens to poor reviews but eventually became a success, although not as big a success as previous works. Suffering from ill health, Fritz goes into retirement.

1973 *Gigi* opens on Broadway.

1975 Fritz is tempted out of retirement by Lerner who shows him the book *The Little Prince* by Antoine de Saint-Exupéry and, together, they begin work to create a simple script and score, but, sadly, the resulting production was their only real flop. Fritz returns to his life of retirement in Palm Springs, California.

1988 Fritz dies on 14 February in Palm Springs, California.

THE MAJOR MILESTONES ON ALAN JAY LERNER'S MUSICAL JOURNEY

1918 Alan Jay Lerner is born on 31 August in New York into a wealthy Manhattan family. He is educated in the UK and then Connecticut before entering Harvard University. During his vacations from Harvard, he also studies at the Juilliard School of Music

1940 He graduates with a B.Sc. degree and goes on to write advertising copy and radio scripts.

1954 He adapts his stage work *Brigadoon* for the screen.

1960 After Fritz went into retirement (both the first time in 1960 and the second time in 1975), Lerner went on writing, continually striving for more hits, but he was only ever to achieve mediocrity in comparison to his successes with Loewe. Sadly, he turned down what could have evolved into his final success, and that was the chance to work with Andrew Lloyd Webber on *The Phantom of the Opera*.

1986 Alan Jay Lerner dies on 14 June of lung cancer in New York.

OVERVIEW

A chance meeting resulted in a partnership that was obviously meant to be, with Lerner and Loewe creating what is arguably one of the best musicals ever written, *My Fair Lady*; a musical that simply won't go away and is continually being professionally revived and for ever the favourite with the amateur societies too.

Frederick Loewe (see page 125)

Richard Maltby Jr (see page 113)

Ivor Novello (see page 103)

Cole Porter

WELL-KNOWN SHOWS

Gay Divorce (1932) • *Anything Goes* (1934) • *Kiss Me Kate* (1948) • *Can Can* (1953) • *Silk Stockings* (1955) • *High Society* (1987)

WELL-KNOWN SONGS

Night and Day (*Gay Divorce*) • I Get a Kick Out of You; You're the Top (*Anything Goes*) • Who Wants to be a Millionaire?; Well Did You Evah?; True Love (*High Society*) • Another Op'nin', Another Show; Brush Up Your Shakespeare; Too Darn Hot; Wunderbar (*Kiss Me Kate*) • C'est Magnifique; I Love Paris; It's All Right With Me (*Can Can*)

THE MAJOR MILESTONES ON COLE PORTER'S MUSICAL JOURNEY

1891	Cole Porter is born on 9 June into a wealthy family in Peru, Indiana; the name Cole is derived from his mother's maiden name, Kate Cole.
1897	Cole starts to learn the piano and the violin; although very good at both, he gives up the violin in favour of the piano, which he practises for two hours a day.
1901	Cole is already composing.
1902	Cole has his first song published.
1905	He enrols at Worcester Academy where he meets with

someone who is to become a great influence on his artistic life, Dr Abercrombie. It was Dr Abercrombie who taught him the valuable lesson about the relationship between words and metre.

1909   Cole begins his life at Yale University where he writes over 300 songs. Some of the football songs he wrote for the students are still sung today.

1913   He attends Harvard Law School, but the pull of music is too great and, after a year, he transfers to the School of Music.

1916   His first Broadway show, *See America First*, is a flop and this hits Cole very hard. It takes him long time to recover and feel ready to return to Broadway.

1919   Cole marries American divorcee, Linda Thomas; it is a business marriage and not a marriage of passion. However, despite the marriage being a sexless union, it is seemingly a happy one.

1928   Cole returns to Broadway and the musical *Paris* is a Broadway hit.

1934   *Anything Goes* opens at the Alvin Theatre.

1937   Cole Fractures both legs in a riding accident, resulting in the eventual amputation of one leg.

1948   *Kiss Me Kate*, which goes on to be Cole Porter's longest running hit show, opens on Broadway.

1958   Cole has his right leg amputated.

1964   Cole Porter dies on 15 October of kidney failure in Santa Monica, California.

OVERVIEW

Unlike most of us, Cole Porter was financially blessed from birth. He was born into a wealthy family and never had to worry about money. This meant that his artistic output was, from the very outset, just that, artistic, and his motivation purely artistic. Money played no part in Cole's reason for writing. He was a flamboyant artist, camp in every sense of the word; a man who would have revelled and delighted in the sexual freedom of the Twenty-first Century, but was born too soon.

Tim Rice

WELL-KNOWN SHOWS

Joseph and the Amazing Technicolor Dream-coat (1968) • *Jesus Christ Superstar* (1971) • *Evita* (1978) • *Blondel* (1983) • *Chess* (1986) • *Beauty and the Beast* (1994) • *The Lion King* (1997) • *Aida* (2002)

WELL-KNOWN SONGS

Any Dream Will Do (*Joseph*) • I Don't Know How to Love Him (*Jesus Christ Superstar*) • Don't Cry For Me Argentina; Another Suitcase in Another Hall (*Evita*) • I Know Him So Well; Heaven Help My Heart (*Chess*) • Can You Feel the Love Tonight; Circle of Life (*The Lion King*)

Tim Rice
Born: 10 November 1944

THE MAJOR MILESTONES ON TIM RICE'S MUSICAL JOURNEY

1944 Tim is born in Amersham, Buckinghamshire. When in his teens, his intention is to become a solicitor, but the pull of the entertainment business is too powerful for him to ignore.

1965 Hearing that Andrew Lloyd Webber is looking for a lyricist, Tim writes to him and a meeting between the two is arranged.

1965 *The Likes of Us* – a musical based on the life of Dr Barnardo, marking the first collaboration between Rice and Lloyd Webber, is written by the pair, however, it is not produced.

1968 Tim begins work as an Assistant Record Producer with the Norrie Paramor Organisation in London.

1968 *Joseph and the Amazing Technicolor Dreamcoat* premières at Colet Court School in London's Hammersmith, with music by Andrew Lloyd Webber and lyrics by Tim Rice; at this stage it is just a 15-minute pop cantata, but is later developed into a full-length stage musical.

1971 *Jesus Christ Superstar* opens on Broadway with music by Andrew Lloyd Webber and lyrics by Tim Rice.

1972 *Jesus Christ Superstar* opens in the West End.

1973 A reworked version of *Joseph*, the shortened version of its full title now in popular usage, opens in the West End.

1974 Tim marries Jane McIntosh from whom he is now separated.

1976 The musical *Evita*, another Lloyd Webber/Rice work, begins its life as a concept album.

1978 *Evita* opens in the West End.

1979 *Evita* opens on Broadway.

1983 *Blondel*, for which Tim collaborated with Stephen Oliver, opens at the Old Vic in London.

1983 *Joseph* opens on Broadway.

1984 The concept album of *Chess* is released, with music by Benny Andersson and Björn Ulvaeus (the ABBA boys).

1986 Andrew Lloyd Webber and Tim Rice write a 30-minute comic musical entitled *Cricket*; this is to celebrate the Queen's 60th birthday. The world première takes place in the presence of HM the Queen and other members of the Royal Family at Windsor Castle – Tim has had a lifelong affair with cricket.

1986 *Chess* opens in the West End.

1991 Disney sign Tim up as a lyricist for *The Lion King*.

1992 He writes the lyrics for the feature film *Aladdin*.

1994 *Beauty and the Beast*, for which Tim wrote the lyrics together with Howard Ashman (music by Alan Menken), opens on Broadway.

1994 Tim is knighted and becomes Sir Tim Rice, a well-deserved honour.

1995 The concept album of the musical *Heathcliff* is released; Tim wrote the lyrics and John Farrar the music.

1997 *The Lion King* opens on Broadway.

1999 Tim is inducted into the Songwriters Hall of Fame.

2000 *Aida* opens on Broadway, the result of the collaboration between Tim and Elton John.

2000 Tim Rice is now the first British writer ever to have four shows playing on Broadway at the same time, these being *Aida*, *Beauty and the Beast*, *The Lion King* and *Jesus Christ Superstar*.

2005 *The Likes of Us*, the first musical Tim wrote with Andrew Lloyd Webber, finally gets its first production at Andrew's Sydmonton – 40 years after it was written.

OVERVIEW

Tim's interests in life are diverse. He is not just knowledgeable and talented in the field of musical theatre, but in many other areas such as cricket, the other great love in his life. Since 1973, he has been running his own cricket team, 'Heartaches CC' taking his first hat-trick in 1987; he has acted as a cricket commentator on the radio and has written a book called the *Treasures of the Lords*. Then there is pop music; he is co-author of the *Guinness Book of Hit Records*; he is also a guest panellist on many radio and TV shows such as *Just a Minute*, *Question Time*, *Mastermind* and *Countdown*. As well as writing for musical theatre, Tim also writes for films (he wrote the lyrics to the song 'All Time High' for the Bond film *Octopussy*), and he writes pop songs. Tim Rice is a talented individual who knows a lot about a lot, making him a much sought-after dinner speaker.

Richard Rodgers, Lorenz Hart and Oscar Hammerstein II

WELL-KNOWN SHOWS

On Your Toes (1936) • *Babes in Arms* (1937) • *Pal Joey* (1940) • *Oklahoma!* (1943) • *Carousel* (1945) • *South Pacific* (1949) • *The King and I* (1951) • *The Sound of Music* (1959)

WELL-KNOWN SONGS

My Funny Valentine; The Lady is a Tramp (*Babes in Arms*) • Falling in Love with Love (*The Boys From Syracuse*) • Bewitched, Bothered and Bewildered (*Pal Joey*) • Oh What a Beautiful Morning; People Will Say We're in Love; The Surrey with the Fringe on Top (*Oklahoma!*) • If I Loved You; You'll Never Walk Alone (*Carousel*) • There is Nothing Like a Dame; Some Enchanted Evening; I'm Gonna Wash That Man Right Outta My Hair (*South Pacific*) • Shall We Dance; Getting to Know You; Hello Young Lovers (*The King and I*) • Do-Re-Mi; Climb Every Mountain; My Favourite Things; Edelweiss (*The Sound of Music*)

THE MAJOR MILESTONES ON RICHARD RODGERS AND LORENZ HART'S MUSICAL JOURNEY

1895	Lorenz Hart is born on 2 May in New York City; he is the eldest of the two sons of Frieda and Max Hart. Fluent in German, he attended the Columbia School of Journalism.
1902	Richard is born Richard Charles Rodgers on the 28 June at Long Island, New York into a doctor's family. He grows up in Upper Manhattan.
1908	Rodgers begins learning to play the piano.
1918	Richard Rodgers and Lorenz Hart first meet up.
1919	Rodgers and Hart make their professional debut with 'Any Old Place with You', featured in the Broadway musical comedy *A Lonely Romeo*.
1925	*The Garrick Gaieties* opens at the Garrick Theatre; it is the first break for Rodgers and Hart.
1926	*The Girlfriend* opens on Broadway with music by Rodgers, lyrics by Hart and book by Herbert Fields.
1927	A rewritten version of *The Girlfriend* opens in the West End.
1930	Rodgers marries Dorothy Feiner.
1932	Rodgers and Hart write the Hollywood film *Love Me Tonight*.
1936	*On Your Toes*, with music by Richard Rodgers, lyrics by Lorenz Hart and book also by Rodgers and Hart together with George Abbott, opens on Broadway; this work includes Rodgers' instrumental ballet, *Slaughter On Tenth Avenue*.
1937	*On Your Toes* opens in the West End.
1937	*Babes in Arms* opens on Broadway with music by Rodgers, lyrics by Hart and book by Rodgers and Hart.
1938	*The Boys From Syracuse* opens in New York. This is the first time Shakespeare has been successfully used as a base. It is a formula that is to be repeated over and over again in the following years.
1940	*Pal Joey*, with music and lyrics by the pair and book by John O'Hara, opens on Broadway with Gene Kelly. It is the first musical comedy to receive the New York Drama Critics Award.
1943	The Rodgers and Hart partnership comes to an end with Lorenz Hart's death on 22 November in New York City.

So while Richard Rodgers was enjoying a successful career with Lorenz Hart, Oscar Hammerstein II was enjoying an equally successful career with other composers.

THE MAJOR MILESTONES ON OSCAR HAMMERSTEIN'S MUSICAL JOURNEY

1895   Oscar Hammerstein II is born on 12 July in New York City into a truly theatrical family; his father is a theatre manager, his Uncle Arthur is a successful Broadway producer and his grandfather a famous opera impresario.

1919   His first play, *The Light*, is produced by his Uncle Arthur; it is a miserable failure, but Oscar is undeterred and carries on regardless.

1924   *Rose Marie* opens in New York with book and lyrics by Otto Harbach and Oscar Hammerstein, and music by Rudolf Friml and Herbert Stothart.

1925   *Rose Marie* opens in the West End.

1926   *The Desert Song* opens on Broadway with the book and lyrics by Otto Harbach, Oscar Hammerstein II and Frank Mandel and music by Sigmund Romberg.

1927   *The Desert Song* opens in the West End.

1927   *Show Boat* opens on Broadway for which Oscar wrote both the book and lyrics, and Jerome Kern the music.

1928   *Show Boat* opens in the West End.

1943   Oscar's final musical before his artistic marriage to Richard Rodgers was *Carmen Jones*, the all-black version of Bizet's opera *Carmen*, which opened on Broadway – although it didn't cross the pond until nearly 60 years later.

1991   *Carmen Jones* opens in the West End.

The time has now come for the start of a partnership that it is to change the face and the very soul of musical theatre for-ever. Musical theatre history is about to be made.

1943   *Oklahoma!* the first collaborative work of Rodgers and Hammerstein opens on Broadway.

1945   Rodgers personal favourite, *Carousel*, opens on Broadway.

1947   *Oklahoma!* opens in the West End.

1949   *South Pacific* opens on Broadway.

1951   *South Pacific* opens in the West End, with Joshua Logan joining Oscar on the book.

1951 *The King and I* opens on Broadway.

1953 *The King and I* opens in the West End.

1953 Rodgers and Hammerstein now have four shows playing simultaneously in New York.

1957 *Cinderella* airs live on television with Julie Andrews in the lead role as Cinderella, with 107 million people watching.

1959 *The Sound of Music* opens on Broadway, with Russell Crouse joining Oscar on the book.

1960 Oscar Hammerstein dies on 23 August of stomach cancer in Doylestown, Pennsylvania. After the death of his partner, Rodgers continues to write with a new generation of writers, including Stephen Sondheim.

1961 *The Sound of Music* opens in the West End.

1979 Rodgers dies on 30 December at the age of 77 in New York City.

OVERVIEW

Rodgers and Hammerstein have been the inspiration for many fledgling writers and are recognised by most as one of the important cornerstones upon which modern musical theatre has been built. To summarise:

- During Richard Rodgers' lifetime he wrote over 900 songs and 40 musicals.
- The last song Rodgers and Hammerstein wrote together was Edelweiss from *The Sound of Music* which was actually written during rehearsals.
- Everyone asks the question, 'What comes first, the music or the lyrics?' In the case of Richard Rodgers his reply would have depended on with whom he was working at the time. When Rodgers worked with Lorenz Hart, he wrote the music first, and then Hart wrote the lyrics. But when he worked with Oscar Hammerstein, Hammerstein wrote the lyrics first and Rodgers wrote music to his lyrics; few modern composers are so readily adaptable.

Claude-Michel Schönberg (see page 112)

Stephen Schwartz

Stephen Schwartz
Born: 6 March 1948

WELL-KNOWN SHOWS

Godspell (1971) • *Pippin* (1972) • *The Baker's Wife* (1976) • *Children of Eden* (1991) • *Pocahontas* (1995) • *The Hunchback of Notre Dame* (1996) • *Wicked* (2003)

WELL-KNOWN SONGS

God Help the Outcasts; Out There (*Hunchback of Notre Dame*) • Colours of the Wind (*Pocahontas*) • Defying Gravity; Popular (*Wicked*) • Day by Day (*Godspell*) • When You Believe (*Prince of Egypt*) • Magic to Do; Corner of the Sky (*Pippin*)

THE MAJOR MILESTONES ON STEPHEN SCHWARTZ'S MUSICAL JOURNEY

1948	Stephen is born on 6 March in New York City. He studies piano and composition at The Juilliard School of Music while still in high school.
1968	Stephen graduates from Carnegie Mellon University with a B.F.A. in Drama and begins working for RCA records in New York City.
1969	He writes the title song for the play *Butterflies are Free,* which is later used in the film version.
1971	*Godspell* the musical, with music and new lyrics by Stephen, opens off Broadway (Cherry Lane Theatre) in May. He is just 23 years old.
1971	He collaborates with Leonard Bernstein to write *Bernstein's Mass,* the landmark piece which inaugurates the Kennedy Center for the Performing Arts in Washington, D.C.
1972	*Godspell* opens in the West End.
1972	*Pippin* the musical opens on Broadway, with music and lyrics by Stephen and book by Roger O. Hirson. Bob Fosse directs.

1974	*The Magic Show*, which goes on to run for five years, opens on Broadway, with music and lyrics by Stephen.
1974	Stephen Schwartz becomes the first composer/lyricist to have three shows running on Broadway at the same time – *Godspell*, *Pippin* and *The Magic Show*.
1978	Stephen adapts and directs the musical *Working*, as well as contributing four songs.
1986	*Rags* the musical opens on Broadway, with lyrics by Stephen, music by Charles Strouse and book by Joseph Stein.
1990	*The Baker's Wife*, with the music and lyrics by Stephen (book by Joseph Stein) and directed by Trevor Nunn, opens in the West End.
1991	*Children of Eden* the musical opens in the West End with music and lyrics by Stephen and book by British director, John Caird.
1995	*Pocahontas* the film is released; Stephen wrote the lyrics, collaborating with Alan Menken who wrote the music.
1996	The film *The Hunchback of Notre Dame* is released for which Stephen and Alan collaborated once more; the film includes that wonderful masterpiece – both musically and lyrically – 'God Help the Outcasts'.
1998	The DreamWorks animated feature *Prince of Egypt* is released, with songs by Stephen.
2000	*The Wonderful World of Disney* TV musical *Geppetto* is aired, with music and lyrics by Stephen.
2003	*Wicked* the musical opens on Broadway, with music and lyrics by Stephen and book by Winnie Holzman.
2006	*Wicked* transfers to the West End of London where it quickly becomes the hottest ticket in town.
2009	Stephen's first opera will première at Opera Santa Barbara. It is based on the 1960s movie, *Séance on a Wet Afternoon*.

OVERVIEW

Not only is Stephen Schwartz a prolific writer, but he is generously and genuinely interested in the future of writing and the struggles of the young people aspiring to follow in his footsteps. Among his contributions to musical theatre, he also runs musical theatre workshops for the American Society of Composers, Authors and Publishers (ASCAP) in New York and

Los Angeles, and he also serves on the ASCAP board as well as being a member of the Council of the Dramatists' Guild.

Stephen Sondheim

WELL-KNOWN SHOWS

West Side Story (1957) • *Gypsy* (1959) • *A Funny Thing Happened On the Way to the Forum* (1962) • *Company* (1970) • *Follies* (1971) • *A Little Night Music* (1973) • *Side by Side by Sondheim* (1976) • *Sweeney Todd* (1979) • *Merrily We Roll Along* (1981) • *Sunday in the Park with George* (1984) • *Into the Woods* (1987) • *Assassins* (1990) • Passion (1994)

Stephen Sondheim
Born: 22 March 1930

WELL-KNOWN SONGS

America; Tonight; Maria; I Feel Pretty; Somewhere (*West Side Story*) • Let Me Entertain You (*Gypsy*) • Send in the Clowns (*A Little Night Music*)

THE MAJOR MILESTONES ON STEPHEN SONDHEIM'S MUSICAL JOURNEY

1930   22 March, Stephen is born in New York, the son of Janet Fox and Herbert Sondheim.

1937   Stephen begins his musical journey when he starts piano lessons.

1940   His parents divorce and he goes to live with his mother in Pennsylvania where his new neighbours just happen to be Oscar Hammerstein II and his family.

1945   Stephen and his friends write their school musical.

1946   Stephen attends Williams College, Massachusetts, to study mathematics.

1947   During a holiday, Stephen takes a job as a gopher on the set of Rodgers and Hammerstein's *Allegro*.

1950   He graduates from Williams College.

1957   *West Side Story*, for which Stephen wrote the lyrics, Leonard

Bernstein wrote the music and Arthur Laurents the book, opens on Broadway.

1959 *Gypsy*, for which Stephen wrote the lyrics, Jule Styne wrote the music and Arthur Laurents the book, opens on Broadway.

1962 A Broadway production of *A Funny Thing Happened On the Way to the Forum* opens, this time with both music and lyrics by Stephen Sondheim, the book was written by Burt Shevelove and Larry Gelbart.

1965 Work begins on *The Girl Upstairs* which, in 1971, evolves into *Follies*.

1970 *Company*, with music and lyrics by Sondheim and book by George Furth, opens on Broadway. It is directed by Hal Prince, as all future Stephen Sondheim works will be up until 1981.

1971 Stephen wins a Grammy Award for Best Score from an Original Cast Show Album for *Company*.

1971 *Follies*, music and lyrics by Sondheim and book by James Goldman, opens on Broadway.

1973 *A Little Night Music*, music and lyrics by Sondheim and book by Hugh Wheeler, opens on Broadway.

1973 *Gypsy* opens in London with lyrics by Sondheim, music by Jule Styne and book by Arthur Laurents.

1975 Judy Collins' recording of 'Send in the Clowns' from *A Little Night Music*, enters into the Billboard Top 50 Chart.

1976 *Pacific Overtures*, with music and lyrics by Sondheim and book by John Weidman (additional material by Hugh Wheeler), opens on Broadway. Hal Prince both produces and directs.

1976 Stephen wins the Grammy Award for Song of the Year for 'Send in the Clowns'.

1976 *Side by Side by Sondheim* (directed by Ned Sherrin), opens in London at the Mermaid Theatre.

1977 *Side by Side by Sondheim* revue opens on Broadway.

1979 *Sweeney Todd*, with music and lyrics by Sondheim and book by Hugh Wheeler, opens on Broadway.

1980 *Sweeney Todd* opens in the West End.

1981 *Merrily We Roll Along* opens on Broadway with music and lyrics by Sondheim and book by George Furth.

1984 *Sunday in the Park with George* opens on Broadway, music and lyrics by Sondheim, book by James Lapine.

1985	Stephen is awarded the Pulitzer Prize for *Sunday in the Park with George.*
1986	British première of *Pacific Overtures* in Manchester.
1987	*Into the Woods* opens on Broadway, with the book by James Lapine.
1987	*Pacific Overtures* opens in the West End.
1990	*Into the Woods* opens in the West End.
1990	*Assassins*, a revue in one act with music and lyrics by Sondheim, opens off Broadway.
1990	*Sunday in the Park with George* opens at the National in London.
1992	The musical revue *Putting It Together* opens in Oxford, England.
1994	*Passion* opens on Broadway, with music and lyrics by Sondheim and book by James Lapine.
2003	*Bounce* with book by John Weidman, the first new Stephen Sondheim musical in nine years, opens at the Eisenhower Theater in Washington. It is also Sondheim's first work with Hal Prince in over 30 years.

OVERVIEW

Stephen Sondheim can never be accused of writing for the mass market; his is, after all, an acquired taste and does not always appeal to the theatre going masses. An actress friend of mine once told me: 'Stephen Sondheim writes for actors, his pieces are so dramatic.' Added to that is the general consensus of opinion that Sondheim writes for himself, for his own gratification, and does not allow public opinion to dictate to him what will appear on his page or on his stage.

Richard Stilgoe

WELL-KNOWN SHOWS

Cats (1981) • *Starlight Express* (1984) • *The Phantom of the Opera* (1986)

WELL-KNOWN SONGS

U.N.C.O.U.P.L.E.D; A Lotta Locomotion; Light at the End of Tunnel (*Starlight Express*) • Jellicle Songs for Jellicle Cats (*Cats*) • The Phantom of the Opera (*The Phantom of the Opera*)

THE MAJOR MILESTONES ON RICHARD STILGOE'S MUSICAL JOURNEY

1943 Richard Henry Simpson Stilgoe is born in Camberley, Surrey, the son of John and Joan Stilgoe.

1946 His family move to Liverpool.

1959 Richard attends Monkton Combe School.

1960 He appears at the Cavern Club, Liverpool, with the Beatles.

1961 Richard goes up to Clare College, Cambridge, where he reads engineering, then music and joins the renowned Cambridge Footlights.

1964 He marries Elizabeth Gross with whom he goes on to have two children.

1975 Now divorced from Elizabeth Gross, Richard marries Annabel Hunt, with whom he goes on to have another three children.

1976 Richard begins his regular appearances on Esther Rantzen's TV series, *That's Life*.

1981 *Cats*, for which Richard wrote some additional lyrics, opens in the West End.

1982 *Cats* opens on Broadway.

1984 *Starlight Express*, for which Richard wrote the lyrics, opens in the West End.

Richard Stilgoe
Born: 28 March 1943

1985 Sees the start of Richard's partnership with Peter Skellern, which continues for 18 years.

1985 Richard founds the Orpheus Trust, a trust which designs and runs music programmes for physically challenged young adults.

1986 *The Phantom of the Opera*, opens in the West End.

1987 *Starlight Express* opens on Broadway.

1987 *Bodywork*, Richard's musical for children premières at the Edinburgh Fringe.

1988 Richard presents the *Schools Proms*.

1991 *Brilliant the Dinosaur*, Richard's second musical for children premières at Chichester Cathedral.

1998 The Orpheus Trust opens a specially designed centre to further their work.

1998 Richard is made High Sheriff of Surrey.

1998 Richard is awarded the OBE for services to the community.

2002 Exit Allan, a musical drama for which Richard wrote the script, is performed at the International Festival of Musicals in Cardiff.

2005 He is appointed President of Surrey Cricket Club, a passion for cricket which he shares with the lyricist Sir Tim Rice.

OVERVIEW

Richard Stilgoe is one of life's 'good men'. His work at the Orpheus Centre has impacted the lives of numerous people who have not been blessed with the health and opportunities of the majority. Mike Hopson, an Orpheus apprentice, was in a wheelchair and found speaking very difficult. He said: 'I don't want to walk and talk; I want to sing and dance!' Mike died in 2007, but not before he had done a lot of singing and dancing. Richard's understated generosity has also bene-fited those outside the UK, for example, he gave away some of his royalties for *Starlight Express* to a village in India. In addition to his 'special work', Richard is a hugely accomplished wordsmith who has made over 200 appearances on the television programme, *Countdown*.

Orpheus Centre

Lord Andrew Lloyd-Webber (see page 7)

Chapter Five

Screen Musicals

Stage v. Screen

UP TO this point, we have looked primarily at stage musicals, but film musicals are as much a part of musical 'theatre' as stage musicals. Some wouldn't agree, however, the fact is that a stage musical may have started its life as a film musical and vice versa; either way, it is a musical. No one knows which films are going to be dragged out of the archives to be resurrected onto the stage in the not too distant future. Similarly, when a theatre can be seen to be packing in the audiences, which film producer will be having his own screen version flashing before their eyes?

Stage v. Screen, which is the best; which wins the prize? Neither! There is no winner because there is no contest. Both have their place in the world of musicals, as the artistic requirements for both are so different and diverse that both have a valid and worthwhile contribution to make.

For some, nothing can compare to the immediacy of live theatre, from the adrenaline rush it gives to its performers knowing that they have only one chance to get it right, to the excitement an audience derives as it watches the complicated dance routines or aerial tricks – that perhaps just may not work that night. On the other hand, the film lover enjoys the near perfect performances possible as a result of the luxury of being able to re-shoot anything less than perfect. Film, with the help of technology, can also create that which cannot be created in a box. But does this matter? Surely a musical is a musical, whatever the medium used?

Which Came First, the Film Version or the Stage Version?

Which came first, the film version or the stage version of a particular musical? It is a question I have been asked more times than I care to remember and so must be of interest to many people; in fact, several of my own thespian friends have actually requested that I include just such a section in this book. So to them and to all the others who are interested, here it is, a quick chicken and egg guide.

On the left hand side of the table is a list of some of the most memorable musical films; the right hand side tells you whether there is a stage version. The **bold** text indicates the form in which a musical first appeared; ~~~~ means that no one has done it yet! So now's your chance!

YEAR	FILM	YEAR	THEATRE
1927	*The Jazz Singer*	~~~~	~~~~
1930	*No, No, Nanette*	**1925**	**West End**
1933	**42nd Street**	1980	Broadway
1936	*Show Boat*	**1927**	**Broadway**
1938	*Alexander's Ragtime Band*	~~~~	~~~~
1939	*Babes in Arms*	**1937**	**New York (Schubert Theatre)**
1939	*The Wizard of Oz*	**1903**	**Broadway**
1941	*Lady be Good*	**1924**	**Broadway**
1943	**Girl Crazy**	1992	Broadway (adaptation)
1944	**Meet Me in St Louis**	1989	Broadway
1945	**State Fair**	1996	Broadway
1948	*Easter Parade*	~~~~	~~~~
1949	*On the Town*	**1944**	**Broadway**
1950	*Annie Get Your Gun*	**1946**	**Broadway**
1952	**Singin' in the Rain**	1983	West End
1953	**Calamity Jane**	1979	West End
1953	*Kiss Me Kate*	**1948**	**Broadway**
1954	*Brigadoon*	**1947**	**Broadway**
1955	*Guys and Dolls*	**1950**	**Broadway**
1955	*Oklahoma!*	**1943**	**Broadway**
1956	*Anything Goes*	**1934**	**Broadway**
1956	**High Society**	1987	West End
1956	*The King and I*	**1951**	**Broadway**
1957	*Funny Face*	~~~~	~~~~
1957	**Jailhouse Rock**	2004	West End
1957	*The Pajama Game*	**1954**	**Broadway**
1957	*Pal Joey*	**1940**	**West End**
1958	**Gigi**	1973	Broadway
1958	*South Pacific*	**1949**	**Broadway**
1960	*Can Can*	**1953**	**Broadway**
1961	*Flower Drum Song*	**1958**	**Broadway**
1961	*West Side Story*	**1957**	**Broadway**
1962	*Gypsy*	**1959**	**Broadway**

YEAR	FILM	YEAR	THEATRE
1962	*The Music Man*	**1957**	**Broadway**
1963	*Bye Bye Birdie*	**1960**	**Broadway**
1964	***Mary Poppins***	2004	West End
1964	*My Fair Lady*	**1956**	**Broadway**
1965	*The Sound of Music*	**1959**	**Broadway**
1967	*Camelot*	**1960**	**Broadway**
1967	*The Jungle Book*	~~~~	~~~~
1967	***Thoroughly Modern Millie***	2002	Broadway
1968	***Chitty Chitty Bang Bang***	2002	West End
1968	*Oliver!*	**1960**	**West End**
1969	*Hello Dolly*	**1964**	**Broadway**
1969	*Paint Your Wagon*	**1951**	**Broadway**
1969	*Sweet Charity*	**1966**	**Broadway**
1970	**Scrooge**	1992	British Provinces
1971	*Bedknobs and Broomsticks*	~~~~	~~~~
1971	*Fiddler On the Roof*	**1964**	**Broadway**
1972	*Cabaret*	**1966**	**Broadway**
1973	*Godspell*	**1971**	**Off Broadway**
1973	*Jesus Christ Superstar*	**1971**	**Broadway**
1975	**Tommy**	1979	West End
1977	***Saturday Night Fever***	1998	West End
1977	*A Little Night Music*	**1973**	**Broadway**
1978	*Grease*	**1972**	**Broadway**
1978	*The Wiz*	**1975**	**Broadway**
1979	*Hair*	**1967**	**Off Broadway**
1982	*Annie*	**1977**	**Broadway**
1982	*The Best Little Whorehouse in Texas*	**1978**	**Broadway**
1985	*A Chorus Line*	**1975**	**Broadway**
1986	*The Little Shop of Horrors*	**1982**	**Off Broadway**
1989	**The Little Mermaid**	2007	Broadway
1991	***Beauty and the Beast***	1994	Broadway
2000	*Joseph and the Amazing Technicolor Dreamcoat*	**1973**	**West End** *(Many versions were) staged in London & Edinburgh betwen 1968 & 1973)*
2006	***High School Musical***	2006	Broadway

A Closer Look at a Few Film Musicals Which Inspired Later Stage Versions

42ND STREET (1933) [Warner Brothers]
Music and Lyrics: Harry Warren & Al Dubin
Starring: Dick Powell, Ruby Keeler

This film takes a behind the scenes look at the making of a Broadway musical and features the spectacular routines of Busby Berkeley, as well as featuring an early appearance by Ginger Rogers.

GIRL CRAZY (1943) [MGM]
Music: George Gershwin **Lyrics:** Ira Gershwin
Starring: Mickey Rooney, Judy Garland

Danny, the son of a newspaper magnate, is getting a reputation as a bit of a playboy and so is sent away by his father to an all boys' school. There might be no girls among the pupils, but the Dean has a granddaughter with whom he quickly falls in love.

This film re-emerges years later in the adapted stage version under the title Crazy For You.

MEET ME IN ST LOUIS (1944) [MGM]
Songs by: Hugh Martin & Ralph Blane
Starring: Judy Garland

Set at the turn of the Twentieth Century, a wealthy family – the Smiths – are faced with the prospect of uprooting and moving to New York. 17-year-old Esther, who has fallen in love with the boy next door, is not pleased at the prospect of this move, despite the fact that he barely notices her.

This charming film took over 50 years to reach the stage.

STATE FAIR (1945) [20th Century Fox]
Music: Richard Rodgers **Lyrics:** Oscar Hammerstein II
Starring: Jeanne Crain, Dana Andrews, Vivian Blaine, Dick Haymes and Charles Winninger

This simple film tells us the story of a family's annual trip to the State Fair.

This is the only original film score by Rodgers and Hammerstein. The film enjoys another remake in 1962 by 20th Century Fox, this time, starring Ann Margaret.

SINGIN' IN THE RAIN (1952) [MGM]
Music: Nacio Herb Brown **Lyrics:** Arthur Freed
Starring: Debbie Reynolds, Gene Kelly and Donald O'Connor
This iconic film takes a rise out of the technical problems endured by the early talkies.

One of the best of what is known as 'The Golden Age of Musicals', Singin' in the Rain is without doubt THE musical which introduced many children to the magical world of musical theatre.

CALAMITY JANE (1953) [Warner Brothers]
Music: Sammy Fain **Lyrics:** Paul Francis Webster
Starring: Doris Day, Howard Keel
Calamity Jane is a tomboy who learns to behave and act like a conventional woman and as a result wins the love of her man – not that she was ever trying to do this as she didn't know that she was in love with him in the first place!

HIGH SOCIETY (1956) [MGM]
Songs: Cole Porter
Starring: Grace Kelly, Bing Crosby, Frank Sinatra,
Louis Armstrong
This is a standard love story in which the girl must choose between the two men in her life – which one is to be her true love?

Grace Kelly was loved, envied and admired by the world and this was, sadly, her last film. Just as with Meet Me in St Louis, *the film took a long time to reach the stage, not arriving until 1987.*

JAILHOUSE ROCK (1957) [MGM]
Songs by: Mike Stoller, Jerry Leiber
Additional Songs: Roy C. Bennett, Aaron Schroeder, Abner Silver,
Sid Tepper, Ben Weisman
Starring: Elvis Presley
The story of a young man who is jailed for killing a woman's attacker and, while serving his sentence, is taught to play the guitar by another inmate. As a consequence, when he is released from jail, he becomes a recording star.

It took until 1994 to bring this musical to the stage and even then, ironically, the producers couldn't get the rights to incorporate the song 'Jailhouse Rock' into the production!

GIGI (1958) [MGM]
Music: Frederick Loewe **Screenplay & Lyrics:** Alan Jay Lerner
Starring: Leslie Caron, Maurice Chevalier, Louis Jordan
It is Twentieth Century Paris and Gigi is growing into a young woman, ably guided by her aunt, when a young man who is a family friend – and unfortunately a playboy – begins to see her in a different light.

MARY POPPINS (1964) [Disney]
Music & Lyrics: Richard Sherman & Robert Sherman
Starring: Julie Andrews, Dick Van Dyke
Set somewhere in London at the turn of the last century where a magical Nanny is brought into a household to control and teach manners to two naughty children.
Cameron Mackintosh first tried to get the rights to bring Mary Poppins *to the stage 25 years before he finally succeeded.*

THOROUGHLY MODERN MILLIE (1967) [Universal]
Music & Lyrics: Sammy Cahn, James 'Jimmy' Van Heusen,
Sylvia Neufield, Jay Thompson
Starring: Julie Andrews, Mary Tyler Moore, Carol Channing
Ambitious Millie intends to marry her boss, but other people have their own ideas! There is a white slave trade story interwoven in the main plot, but the best part is trying to spot the hidden references to films from the 1920s – one for the knowledgeable film buff.
Another long journey to the stage, this took until 2002.

SCROOGE (1970) [Waterbury Films/National General (UK)]
Music & Lyrics: Leslie Bricusse
Starring: Albert Finney, Alec Guinness, Edith Evans, Kenneth Moore
The story of Scrooge is taken directly from Charles Dickens' novel, *A Christmas Carol*.

TOMMY (1975) [Columbia]
Song Score: Roger Daltrey, John Entwistle, Keith Moon and
Pete Townshend
'Eyesight to the Blind' by Sonny Boy Williamson
Starring: Oliver Reed, Ann Margaret, Roger Daltrey, Elton John
This is the story of a deaf, dumb and blind boy who is a whiz on the pinball machine.

SATURDAY NIGHT FEVER (1977) [Paramount]
Original Music by: Barry Gibb, Maurice Gibb, Robin Gibb
(The Bee Gees)
Starring: John Travolta

The highlight of Tony's life is the local disco where he is King of the dance floor. It is here that he meets Stephanie and they agree to dance together in a competition and so their lives become entwined.

BEAUTY AND THE BEAST (1991)
[Silver Screen Partners IV/Walt Disney Productions/Buena Vista]
Music: Alan Menken **Lyrics:** Howard Ashman
= Animated=

Belle is a beautiful, educated, young woman who falls in love with a ferocious and ugly Beast, thus breaking the spell cast upon him to lead his life as a Beast until he learns the meaning of real love.

A Brief History of the Film Musical After 1920

I think it is only right and fair to state the obvious at this point and that is that, in terms of the film industry, Hollywood Rules! Of course the UK have made some excellent films over the years, but there is no getting away from the fact that films and Hollywood walk hand in hand.

1920s

The 1920s and Hollywood is in chaos; sound has arrived in an otherwise silent industry and, to begin with, it is an unwanted visitor. But, like all unwanted visitors, it just refuses to go away and keeps knocking at the door. The irony is that the film executives were not interested in the actors talking, but rather could see the dramatic possibilities to be gained from the use of music as a background effect. Audiences of the 1920s, however, had other ideas; they wanted sound on the screen. As the majority generally talks sense and wins the war of words, then it is fair to say that sound on the screen was inevitable. Since that time, when advancement often met with resistance, things have improved somewhat and we now readily court and embrace new concepts meaning that, in the last 20 years, we have forged ahead in every way.

The Jazz Singer **[Warner Brothers 1927]** starring Al Jolson, was the first full-length feature film to use recorded song and dialogue. However, despite this, it was still a fairly silent film with no actual dialogue planned.

But Al Jolson started to ad lib around his songs, which was when he uttered those immortal words: 'You aint heard nothin' yet!'

The Jazz Singer was an amazing success, despite most cinemas not being equipped for sound, necessitating that the audiences watch the talkie in silence! Nothing, however, was going to stop this runaway train and sound was here to stay. *The Jazz Singer* was remade twice, once in 1953 with the great Peggy Lee and Danny Thomas and again in 1980, this time starring Neil Diamond and Sir Laurence Olivier.

The talkies got bigger and better and the world of the screen musical arrived to coincide with the acceleration of the stage musicals. To sum up, the 1920s, although not the decade which gave birth to musicals, was certainly the decade responsible for the early nurturing process, both on stage and screen.

1930s

With the advent of the 1930s, the screen musical began in earnest producing not only wonderful film musicals, but flamboyant and innovative directors and creators too. Most people have heard of possibly the greatest dance director of all time, Busby Berkeley. He choreographed not only the dancers themselves but the cameras too, for he believed that the camera was not just the eye of the audience but was, in fact, an integral part of each number he staged; he was a cinematic genius. Sadly, personal problems eroded his mental stability and he became a victim of alcohol, the demon of many an artistic genius, which in turn led to other problems. As a result, his career came to a premature end, the loss being not only to Busby Berkeley himself but to the cinema going millions and to the world of musical 'theatre'.

At this time, there came into being a code of conduct on screen, examples of which are:

- During a screen hug, one actor must always have at least one foot firmly on the ground.
- Actors may not share a bed on screen.
- Kisses had to be closed mouthed and with a time limit of six seconds.

This code of conduct, known as the 'Production Code' was strictly enforced from the mid-1930s to the mid-1960s and had a huge impact on Hollywood.

Then, just at a time when contrived (directed) sexual chemistry was forbidden on screen there came along two performers who exuded the forbidden fruit naturally, it seemed, from every pore in their body; of course they were the great team of Fred Astaire and Ginger Rogers. And how did they do it? Through the innocent form of dance! Additionally, it was their partnership which began to use the medium of dance in order to advance the plot, previously unheard of, for dance was just thought to be, well, dance!

Those who are musical screen buffs will be familiar with the magic of the following films and their dance sequences:

Follow the Fleet (1936)	– with 'Let's Face the Music and Dance' (Irving Berlin)
Swing Time (1936)	– with 'The Way You Look Tonight' (Jerome Kern)
Shall We Dance (1937)	– with 'Let's Call the Whole Thing Off' (George and Ira Gershwin) 'They Can't Take That Away From Me' (George and Ira Gershwin)

Aside from Fred Astaire and Ginger Rogers, Hollywood film musicals of the 1930s were a thriving business, providing the romantic escapism the world needed at this time, just as the stage musicals were doing in the theatres.

Another light relief came in the form of the wonderful Shirley Temple, who delighted adults and children alike with her own special form of magic; who could resist a cute tot singing and dancing to perfection, and one with dimples and curls too? Not the audiences of the 1930s, that's for sure and so Shirley Temple became big box office.

Then Disney entered the world of musicals – animated musicals – with *Snow White and the Seven Dwarfs* (1937) giving us such memorable songs as 'Heigh-Ho' and 'Some Day My Prince Will Come'.

Of course, we can end this decade on one film only and that is *The Wizard of Oz* (1939). Never before or since has a film been so widely known and loved; stop anyone in any street and ask them to tell you the story of *The Wizard of Oz* – and they will! MGM wanted to borrow Shirley Temple from Fox to play the part of Dorothy Gale, but MGM refused and so the part went to second choice, Judy Garland.

1940s

In this decade, just as the world turned to the stage for light relief from what was going on around them in the terms of the death and destruction of the Second World War, so too did they turn to the cinema, where Hollywood in particular, did not let them down.

The world of entertainment is often seen as a somewhat flippant world. And arguably it is. However, it does make peoples' lives a little easier in times of trouble and this it did to great effect in the 1940s. Many Hollywood stars were in active service during the war, whilst others entertained the troops – a tradition that continues to this day in times of trouble.

This decade gave us great musical stars in the guise of Bing Crosby and Danny Kaye, and saw the 1942 film *Holiday Inn* (where Bing Crosby teamed up with Fred Astaire) bring Irving Berlin's captivating songs to the world including 'White Christmas', which was to become the best-selling single of all time until it eventually lost this position five decades later to Elton John's tribute song to Princess Diana, 'Candle in the Wind 1997'.

Another huge hit of the 1940s was *Cover Girl* (1944), featuring Rita Hayworth (though her singing was always dubbed) and Gene Kelly. This film gave us the famous 'alter ego' dance with a reflection of himself in a glass window.

Interestingly, it was the 1940s which gave us the only Rodgers and Hammerstein musical written directly for the big screen, *State Fair* (1945) featuring the show-stopping songs 'It's a Grand Night for Singing' and 'It Might as Well be Spring'.

1950s

On the horizon, however, was the bullet that would kill the big blockbuster screen musicals – television. Who in their right mind would leave a comfortable home to watch a film in a room shared with hundreds of other people; less and less it would seem, for cinema going audiences dropped dramatically during this decade. It wasn't all doom and gloom though because Rodgers and Hammerstein's stage hits, *Oklahoma!* (1955), *Carousel* (1956), *The King and I* (1956) and *South Pacific* (1958) were all adapted and turned into highly successful films. Even then, audiences would brave the cold and discomfort to watch a musical.

As far as the actors and actresses themselves were concerned, there was another darling of the musical screen who came to the forefront in this decade and this was the wholesome, all-American girl with the crystal clear voice, Doris Day. Even today, although many young people don't actually know who she is, I only have to play a recording of her and they immediately want to sing like her.

Walt Disney also continued his musical, animated films with *Cinderella* (1950), *Alice in Wonderland* (1951), *Peter Pan* (1953), *The Lady and the Tramp* (1955) and *Sleeping Beauty* (1959) as Hollywood went on to produce some of the finest musicals of all time:

Kiss Me Kate (1953)	– an adaptation of Cole Porter's stage show
High Society (1956)	– with a score by Cole Porter
Singin' in the Rain (1952)	– and who doesn't know the sequence which features a rain-drenched Gene Kelly swinging from a lamppost singing the title tune?
Seven Brides for Seven Brothers (1957)	– remembered for the spectacular dance routines which involved athletic dancers and a great many planks of wood! Interestingly, *Seven Brides for Seven Brothers* had a totally original score whereas other screen musicals used recycled songs from previous stage or screen projects.

The silver screen was dying – in terms of audience – but it was refusing to die quietly. It went on to give us, among other musical films, the touching and remarkable musical film *Gigi* (1959).

1960s

Despite the depletion in audience numbers, this decade was set to make and break box office records – for Julie Andrews had arrived. At first, she was rejected by Hollywood when Jack Warner of Warner Brothers thought her not 'photogenic' enough to play the part of Eliza Doolittle in the musical film version of the Broadway show *My Fair Lady*; a part Andrews herself had created for the stage and which then went to Audrey Hepburn in the film. Hepburn did not have the vocal abilities of Julie Andrews and so her song vocals were dubbed, however, no one could criticise her performance. Julie Andrews then went on to make two huge audience magnets, *Mary Poppins* (1964) and *The Sound of Music* (1965), the latter of which was to become one of the highest grossing musicals of all time.

Other big musicals of this decade were *West Side Story* (1961) and *Oliver!* (1968), these two films, along with *The Sound of Music*, were thought by some to be better than their original stage versions.

We cannot close this decade without mentioning Elvis Presley who, from a period in the late-1950s to 1970, made over 30 musical films. These films, however, can only be called musical because Elvis sang in them. They were actually more of a vehicle for his talent than a reflection of true musical films; it is also reported that he himself did not enjoy making these plot-weary films.

1970s

When you've 'climb(ed) every mountain' as the musicals of the 1960s had done, then the only way is down; and down we went in the 1970s, into an artistically barren hole. There was the odd oasis on the horizon with the likes of *Fiddler On the Roof* (1971) and *Cabaret* (1972) but, on the whole, the only hope was to leave this decade behind as quickly and quietly as possible. This was not possible though because, out of the fog, came *Grease* (1978) to save the reputation of the decade; it came and it stayed to be replayed *ad nauseam* by what seemed to be a never-ending stream of early-teen youngsters, all eager to prove they were street-wise – and so it goes on, even today.

1980s

The 1980s were no better and things were not looking too good until two musicals did save the day – or rather the decade. They were *The Little Shop of Horrors* (1986) and *The Little Mermaid* (1989), the latter being the first animated musical in decades. Its success was to point the way for future animated musicals, which were set to gross Disney millions and thrill adults and children alike with their quirky singing animations.

1990s

It was the more and more ambitious animated musicals that were to make their indelible mark on the 1990s. Audiences now had more sophisticated taste and their expectations were greater; in this consumer society, they wanted perfection all round and the film industry was no exception to this. They were expected to deliver and deliver they did – in abundance, in the first half of the decade at least. 1991 saw Disney's animated musical *Beauty and the Beast* gain the worldwide acclaim it so rightly deserved. Sadly though, the premature death of Howard Ashman, the lyricist of this masterpiece, cast a dark cloud over its colourful success. Now we can only speculate as to the great things the extraordinary writing team of Howard Ashman and his partner, composer Alan Menken, might have achieved had Ashman lived longer. He did, however, leave us a partially finished *Aladdin* (1992), for which Tim Rice went on to complete the lyrics.

It seemed then that animation was set for world domination as there quickly followed *The Lion King* (1994), with music by Elton John and lyrics by Tim Rice and *Pocahontas* (1995), this time with music by Alan Menken and lyrics by Stephen Schwartz. The Menken and Schwartz partnership followed *Pocahontas* with *The Hunchback of Notre Dame* (1996). Then, as suddenly as it began, the animated musical appeared to peak. There was only one way it could go and, sadly, that was downhill, and so off we went once more on that slippery downhill slide. The animation *Hercules* (1997) by Alan Menken and David Zippel failed to enjoy the success of its predecessors as did *Mulan* (1998) and *Tarzan* (1999). And what of the non-animated musical films in this decade? We did eventually see the long-awaited film version of Andrew Lloyd Webber's stage musical *Evita* hit the screen, starring Madonna; sadly, though, not to critical acclaim. And so this decade, which started so well, limped to a close and we moved on to another century.

2000s

Things did not look too promising. We had *Moulin Rouge* (2001), which did nothing to excite anyone and then along came *Chicago* (2002), which the purists loved but which seemed to bypass the all-important 'man in the street'. The film version of Andrew Lloyd Webber's *The Phantom of the Opera* (2005) did nothing to convince us that there was 'Light at the end of the tunnel' (*Starlight Express*) and so we found ourselves past the midway mark of the decade waiting for someone to light the flame again. Who knows when this will happen, or indeed whether it will at all; we can but wait and see, and hope. But, if history is anything to go, by then we will soon 'Pick ourselves up, dust ourselves down, and start all over again' – Jerome Kern (music), Dorothy Fields (lyrics).

The Golden People from the Golden Age of Film Musicals

Hollywood has produced some wonderful films over the years and those films have been a breeding ground for individuals who have come to be known as film stars. For some reason, the film industry breeds stars in a way that the theatre does not. This seems to have nothing to do with talent but is more a result of the vast amounts of money the film industry is able to throw at its stars, money which is not available in theatre-land. Stars of years gone by tended to be more durable; not only in the film industry but in pop too. Look at the lifers such as Cliff Richard and the Rolling Stones; I can't imagine some of today's pop stars being around in another 50 or so years. The interesting fact is that the youth of today do know about past film stars such as Judy Garland, Frank Sinatra and Gene Kelly and so we will just take a cursory glance at some of these very special 'Golden People'. Although, strictly speaking, not everyone here is from what is commonly known as the Golden Age of film musicals, but surely anyone who makes a prolific contribution to musical theatre, be it on stage or screen, is worthy of the title 'Golden'?

FRED ASTAIRE 1899–1987

Fred Astaire was born Frederick Austerlitz in Omaha, Nebraska. He is the legendary song and dance man of whom it was once said, following a screen test: 'can't sing, can't act; can dance a bit'. Despite the fact that he danced with many different partners he will always be remembered for his partnership with Ginger Rogers.

SOME WELL-KNOWN FILM MUSICALS IN WHICH FRED ASTAIRE APPEARED (PLUS WELL-KNOWN SONGS)

- * *The Gay Divorcee* (1934) – 'Night and Day'
- * *Top Hat* (1935) – 'Cheek to Cheek'
- * *A Damsel in Distress* (1937) – 'Nice Work If You Can Get It'
- * *The Barkleys of Broadway* (1949) – 'They Can't Take That Away From Me'
- *Funny Face* (1957) – 'S'Wonderful'

Those marked with * indicate that the film was made with Ginger Rogers.

BUSBY BERKELEY 1895–1976

Busby Berkeley started his career by directing camp shows for the soldiers when he was in the army. He later discovered that he had a talent for staging large, impressive dance numbers and it was then that he broke with convention and insisted that he not only choreograph the number, but that he be permitted to choose the camera angles too. The result was that he developed a unique way of using camera angles, sometimes even boring holes in the roof to secure those amazing aerial shots for which he became well-known – and so a legend was born. He went on to create some musical masterpieces and, at one point, had 150 girls doing a tap routine for his *pièce de résistance* in *Lullaby of Broadway*.

SOME WELL-KNOWN FILM MUSICALS IN WHICH BUSBY BEREKELEY STAGED HIS DANCE ROUTINES

- *42nd Street* (1933) – 'Shuffle Off to Buffalo'
- *Gold Diggers* (1933) – 'We're in the Money'
- *Hollywood Hotel* (1937) – 'Hooray for Hollywood'

BING CROSBY 1903–1977

Born Harry Lillis Crosby in Tacoma, Washington, the fourth of seven children, his name was later changed to 'Bing'. His early intention was to become a lawyer but, thankfully, he dropped his studies and turned to the world of entertainment. He was a rare artist in that he insisted on singing the words of a song and not merely the tune; too many great singers, past and present, think that all that matters is the melody of a song. Bing, however, appreciated that a melody, which is after all just 'la la la la la', would be shallow and boring without the lyrics. And so every note he sang carried an intention and a meaning as he thoughtfully sang the words – and always in that wonderful laid back style too, a style that no one else has ever quite mastered.

SOME WELL-KNOWN FILM MUSICALS IN WHICH BING CROSBY APPEARED (PLUS WELL-KNOWN SONGS)
- *Rhythm on the Range* (1936) – 'Roundup Lullaby'
- *Anything Goes* (1936) – 'All Through the Night'
- *Holiday Inn* (1942) – 'White Christmas'
- *Going My Way* (1944) – 'Swinging On a Star'

- *White Christmas* (1954) – 'Count Your Blessings Instead of Sheep'
- *High Society* (1956) – 'True Love'

DORIS DAY 1924–

Born Doris Kappelhoff in Ohio, she was the youngest of three children and became known throughout the world for her all-American, wholesome image and crystal clear voice.

SOME WELL-KNOWN FILM MUSICALS IN WHICH DORIS DAY APPEARED (PLUS WELL-KNOWN SONGS)

- *Lullaby of Broadway* (1951) – 'You're Getting to be a Habit with Me'
- *Calamity Jane* (1953) – 'Secret Love'
- *By the Light of the Silvery Moon* (1953) – 'If You Were the Only Girl in the World'
- *Love Me or Leave Me* (1955) – 'You Made Me Love You'
- *The Pajama Game* (1957) – 'Steam Heat'

JUDY GARLAND 1922–1969

Most people know the name of Judy Garland. It is a name synonymous with the evergreen musical *The Wizard of Oz*. But she was so much more than *The Wizard of Oz*. The youngest of three sisters and from a theatrical family, Judy was actually born Frances Ethel Gumm in Minnesota, where she is reputed to have made her stage debut at the age of just two-and-a-half-years-old. She later changed her name to Judy Garland and went on to appear in 16 MGM musicals during the 1940s alone.

SOME WELL-KNOWN FILM MUSICALS IN WHICH JUDY GARLAND APPEARED (PLUS WELL-KNOWN SONGS)

- *The Wizard of Oz* (1939) – 'Somewhere Over the Rainbow'
- *Babes in Arms* (1939) – 'You are My Lucky Star'
- *Strike Up the Band* (1940) – 'Our Love Affair'
- *Girl Crazy* (1943) – 'Embraceable You'
- *Meet Me in St Louis* (1944) – 'The Trolley Song'
- *Easter Parade* (1948) – 'Couple of Swells'
- *A Star is Born* (1954) – 'The Man That Got Away'

GENE KELLY 1912–1997

Gene was born Eugene Curran Kelly in Pittsburgh, Pennsylvania, and grew up to be a dancer, actor, director and choreographer the like of which – along with Fred Astaire – the world of musical theatre had never seen. His style was innovative, creative and easy and, through it, he advanced the popularity of musical theatre.

SOME WELL-KNOWN FILM MUSICALS IN WHICH GENE KELLY APPEARED (PLUS WELL-KNOWN SONGS)

- *Cover Girl* (1944) – 'Long Ago and Far Away'
- *An American in Paris* (1951) – 'I'll Build a Stairway to Paradise'
- *Singin' in the Rain* (1952) – 'You Are My Lucky Star'
- *Brigadoon* (1954) – 'Almost Like being in Love'

DONALD O'CONNOR 1923–2005

Donald O'Connor was born in Chicago, Illinois. He began his professional life in Vaudeville with his family before moving into films. He will be most remembered for his role in *Singin' in the Rain* with Gene Kelly and Debbie Reynolds, which he threw himself into with the unbridled energy that became his trademark.

SOME WELL-KNOWN FILM MUSICALS IN WHICH DONALD O'CONNOR APPEARED (PLUS WELL-KNOWN SONGS)

- *Follow the Boys* (1944) – 'Is You is or is You Ain't (Ma Baby)'
- *Call Me Madam* (1953) – 'It's a Lovely Day Today'
- *There's No Business Like Show Business* (1954) – 'Alexander's Ragtime Band'
- *Anything Goes* (1956) – 'It's D' Lovely'

ELVIS PRESLEY 1935–1977

Elvis was born in Mississippi. Although some would say that Elvis – 'The King' – was a pop star who 'threw' out some films and, therefore, should not be included here, the true fact of the matter is that Elvis was and is, even in death, an icon who made musical films that millions wanted to see.

SOME WELL-KNOWN FILM MUSICALS IN WHICH ELVIS PRESLEY APPEARED (PLUS WELL-KNOWN SONGS)

- *Loving You* (1957) – 'Let Me be Your Teddy Bear'
- *GI Blues* (1960) – 'Wooden Heart'
- *Blue Hawaii* (1961) – 'Rock a Hula Baby'

MICKEY ROONEY 1920–

Mickey was actually born Joe Yule Jr in Brooklyn, New York. During his time as a 'film star' he made over 150 films and, as yet, shows no sign of retiring. Yet, strangely, he is still remembered for his wonderful partnership with the equally legendary Judy Garland, with whom he made just eight films.

SOME WELL-KNOWN FILM MUSICALS IN WHICH MICKEY ROONEY APPEARED (PLUS WELL-KNOWN SONGS)

- *Babes in Arms* (1939) – 'Ida Sweet as Apple Cider/On Moonlight Bay'
- *Girl Crazy* (1943) – 'Bidin' My Time'
- Strike Up the Band (1940) – 'Our Love Affair'

FRANK SINATRA 1915-1998

Frank was born Francis Albert Sinatra in New Jersey, where he grew up as an only child. He was also known by the affectionate name of, Ol' Blue Eyes. An outstanding actor as well as singer, he soon became a heart-throb of his time.

SOME WELL-KNOWN FILM MUSICALS IN WHICH FRANK SINATRA APPEARED (PLUS WELL-KNOWN SONGS)

- *Young at Heart* (1955) – 'Just One of Those Things'
- *Guys and Dolls* (1955) – 'Luck be a Lady'
- *High Society* (1956) – 'Who Wants to be a Millionaire?'
- *Pal Joey* (1957) – 'The Lady is a Tramp'

SHIRLEY TEMPLE 1928–

Surely she must be the most famous and talented child star ever to have graced the silver screen; it wasn't just her talent that wowed everyone but her age, beginning her screen career at four years old. Although most of her films were not strictly musicals, she usually sang and danced in them. The film studios had quickly realised that this curly-haired, dimpled little tot singing and dancing was what the public wanted to see and what, as a result, would make them a lot of money.

SOME WELL-KNOWN FILM MUSICALS IN WHICH SHIRLEY TEMPLE APPEARED (PLUS WELL-KNOWN SONGS)

- *Stand Up and Cheer* (1934) – 'Baby Take a Bow'
- *Little Miss Marker* (1934) – 'Laugh You Son of a Gun'
- *Bright Eyes* (1934) – 'On the Good Ship Lollipop'
- *Curly Top* (1935) – 'Animal Crackers in My Soup'
- *Captain January* (1936) – 'Early Bird'

OTHER GOLDEN PEOPLE
(AND THEIR MOST FAMOUS WORK)

In such a goldmine of greats, one could go on forever and so I have had to be quite strict with myself, however, I have added just a few more here.

JULIE ANDREWS *Mary Poppins (1964), Sound of Music (1965), Thoroughly Modern Millie (1967)*

DICK VAN DYKE *Bye Bye Birdie (1963), Mary Poppins (1964), Chitty Chitty Bang Bang (1968)*

DANNY KAYE *Hans Christian Andersen (1952)*

HOWARD KEEL *Show Boat (1951), Calamity Jane (1953), Seven Brides for Seven Brothers (1954), Kismet (1955)*

DEBORAH KERR *The King and I (1956)*

DEBBIE REYNOLDS *Singin' in the Rain (1952)*

Chapter Six

Well I Never Knew That!

SO WE come to the final curtain and, hopefully, you will know a little more than you did when you started reading this book. So, what could be a better way to round it all off than to entertain you with just a few more strange and interesting facts – after all, that's what it is all about, ENTERTAINMENT!

- Stephen Schwartz wrote the lyrics and new music for *Godspell* in just five weeks.

- Stephen Schwartz wrote his musical *Pippin* while still in college and before he began work on *Godspell* – *Godspell*, however, opened first.

- Bob Fosse was the only director to win a Tony, an Emmy and an Oscar in the same year, (1973). Two Tonys – direction and choreography – for *Pippin*, an Emmy for *Liza with a Z*, an Oscar for *Cabaret*.

- The musical *Anything Goes* started out life as the musical *Bon Voyage*.

- Judy Garland was working on the film musical *Annie Get Your Gun* when she was suspended from MGM.

- *The Great White Way* is so-called because of all the neon lights from the theatres on Broadway.

- The first ever performance of *Joseph and the Amazing Technicolor Dreamcoat* was at Colet Court School, London, and was just a 15-minute long cantata.

- Until she snapped her Achilles' tendon in rehearsal, Dame Judi Dench was set to play the part of Grizabella in the musical *Cats*.

- Tim Rice has actually played the part of the Pharaoh in his own production of *Joseph and the Amazing Technicolor Dreamcoat*.

- There are more than 200 puppets in the show *The Lion King*.

- A skater in *Starlight Express* reached a speed of 40 miles an hour during one rehearsal.

- The Savoy Theatre was the first theatre in the world to be lit entirely by electric lights.

- 'Let Us Love in Peace' from *The Beautiful Game* was used as the closing song at the service for families of the World Trade Center atrocity in October 2001.

- Each performance of *The Phantom of the Opera* has 230 costumes, 14 dressers, 120 automated cues, 22 scene changes, 281 candles, 10 fog and smoke machines and uses 250kg of dry ice.

- When Trevor Nunn spoke out against the use of the term 'luvvie' in Britain, which he regarded as insulting to thespians, the satirical magazine *Private Eye* took to calling its 'Luvvies' section 'Trevvies'.

- In the song, 'The Surrey with the Fringe On Top', from the musical *Oklahoma!* Richard Rodgers used repeated notes in the chorus to indicate a ride on a long flat road.

- An Early Review for *Oklahoma!* 'No gags, no girls, no chance'!

- W.S. Gilbert died while saving a young woman from drowning in a lake on his estate.

- W.S. Gilbert once wrote humorous verses for popular magazines under the nickname 'Bab'.

- By the time he was eight years old Arthur Sullivan (Gilbert and Sullivan) could play every instrument in the military band of which his father was the bandmaster.

- Jerome Kern was originally hired to write the score for *Annie Get Your Gun* but died before he was able to start work on the score; he was replaced by Irving Berlin.

- On Friday 19 November 2004 the lights in all Broadway theatres were dimmed in honour and memory of Cy Coleman.

- MGM executives wanted the song 'Somewhere Over the Rainbow' to be cut from the musical film *The Wizard of Oz*.

Two Final Points to Bear in Mind

'Keep going to the theatre – keep writing – keep performing.
This little **business** we call **show**
is very alive but does still need nurturing.'
Mike Dixon

And to all you budding thespians remember:
It's nice to be important,
But it's more important to be nice.

THE END

Sources and Bibliography

Evans, M., *Musicals: Facts Figures & Fun* (Facts, Figures & Fun, 2006)
Everett, W.A. and Laird, P.R. (Eds), *The Cambridge Companion to the Musical* (Cambridge University Press, 2002)
Gänzl, K., *Musicals* (Carlton Books Ltd, 2004)
Green, S., *Encyclopedia of the Musical Theatre* (Da Capo Press, 1976)
Jackson, A., *The Book of Musicals* (Mitchell Beazley, 1977)
Larkin, C., *The Encyclopedia of Stage and Film Musicals* (Virgin, 2000)

www.britannia.com
www.classicmoviemusicals.com
www.dorothyfields.co.uk
www.math.boisetates.edu/GaS/
www.musicals101.com
www.nodanw.com
www.stageagent.com

Acknowledgements

MY THANKS go first to those I love, those who make my world go 'round', my patient family: Gwyn, my husband, who has been banned from the computer for months on end; Kieran, my son, who spends his life driving to see me because I never seem to have the time to drive to him; Vicky, my daughter, for it is off her I bounce all my ideas and it is her who advises me on content; and then there are my adorable grandchildren, Aaron, Kristian, Ellis and Harry for just being adorable; Paula and Aisha for their continued love and support; Michael, my erudite cousin whom I rely upon to dig me out of the 'dumb' holes into which I seem to regularly tumble.

My thanks also must go to my agent Hilary at Straight Line Management who is more than 'just an agent', she is my friend too and helps me out on the more mundane aspects of research, and to Jo my childhood friend whose loyalty and patience never wanes.

Thanks to must also go to: Adam Gershwin (George Gershwin Family Trust), Arlo Chan (Warner Chappell), Cameron Mackintosh Ltd, Jason Robert Brown, John Alduous, L.J. Strunsky and Michael Owen (Ira and Leonore Gershwin Trust), Lynne Chapman (Stephen Sondheim Society), Michael Cole (PA to Stephen Schwartz), Neil Smith (G&S Archive), Richard Jordon, the Orpheus Centre.

And finally to my Mother, whose love, devotion and words of wisdom always have and always will drive my life forward.

Permissions

FOR THE permission to publish the images that appear in this book I would like to thank the following:

L.B. Photography for the photo of Richard Jordan on p. ix

Laine Theatre Arts and Laura Stanfield for their kind permission to reproduce the image of the Chorus Line on p. 4

John Swannell for the photo of Lord Lloyd-Webber on p. 8

Michael Le Poer Trench for the photo of Sir Cameron Mackintosh on p. 14, Claude-Michel Schönberg on p. 111 and Lionel Bart on p. 105

York Festival Trust (www.yorkmysteryplays.co.uk) for the image of the York Mystery Plays on p. 20

The G&S Archive for their kind permission to reproduce the photos of Gilbert and Sullivan on pp. 22 and 23, and cartoons and posters from their works on pp. 27, 28, 29, 30, 31, 32, 33

The photo of Alain Boubil on p. 111 is reproduced with his own kind permission

Carl van Vechten – Library of Congress, Prints and Photographs Division, Ven Vechten Collection, repro no. LC-USZ62-42534 for the photo of George Gershwin on p. 118.

The photo of Ira Gershwin on p. 118 is provided courtesy of the Ira and Leonore Gershwin Trusts

Jerry Jackson for the photo of Stephen Sondheim on p. 137

Joan Lauren for the photo of Stephen Schwartz on p. 135

Andy Rice for the photo of Tim Rice on p. 129

The Orpheus Centre for the kind permission to reproduce the photos of Richard Stilgoe and the Orpheus Centre itself on pp. 140 and 141

Steven Sherman for the photo of Jason Robert Brown on p. 113

The photo of Sir Elton John on p. 121 is provided courtesy of the Elton John archive.

Index

Index

Index

Index